Growing up
with
Subbuteo

Growing up with Subbuteo

*My Dad invented the
world's greatest football game*

Mark Adolph

SPORTS
BOOKS

Published by SportsBooks Ltd

Copyright: © Mark Adolph
October 2006

SportsBooks Limited
PO Box 422
Cheltenham
GL50 2YN
United Kingdom
Tel: 01242 256755
Fax: 01242 254694
e-mail   randall@sportsbooks.ltd.uk
Website www.sportsbooks.ltd.uk

Cover by Kath Northam

A CIP catalogue record for this book is available from the British Library.

ISBN 1899807 40 3
Printed by Cromwell Press

Dedicated to my father
Peter Arthur Adolph
7th December 1916
to
17th March 1994

ACKNOWLEDGEMENTS

With thanks to: Anthony Adolph, my cousin, author, broadcaster and genealogist; Richard Watt for being such a magnificent opponent in the early days; David Ward for his encouragement and ideas; Chris and Ingrid Tarrant for their advice on finding a publisher; Tony Crook at Bristol Cars for his painstaking research into his archives; Microsoft 3D Pinball for getting me to sit at my computer in the first place!

Also to Ian Woods and Rachel Craven at Hasbro UK for the use of the Subbuteo logo; Michael (Mick) Hill for his advice and ornithological expertise; Richard Payne for allowing me access to his Subbuteo knowledge.

Finally, to my wife Nikki, my daughter Lauren and my son Tom for their love, support, belief and encouragement and being there to kick me when I need it most!

CONTENTS

Introduction

MOST PEOPLE IN the civilised world have heard of Subbuteo. That is not an immodest claim. It is one of those words which for some reason seems to permeate the subconscious mind and become lodged there for ever. It might be known by somebody who knows of someone who owns a Subbuteo set, but has never indulged in playing the game themselves or someone who from a very early age spent all their spare time kneeling on the floor flicking little plastic men at a plastic football. If they are lucky, they might even have been playing on a table, thus avoiding sore knees, backache and having players snapped off at the ankles due to someone's misplaced body part while crawling around on the floor. Every single one of these people always seems to have very fond memories of Subbuteo, be it friendly, or sometimes not so friendly, squabbles over a disallowed goal during their recreation of a real-life cup final, or when Accrington Stanley beat Brazil 5-0. These anecdotes are endless and everyone has a story to tell.

I, too, have a story to tell, for it was my late father, Peter Arthur Adolph, who invented the game of Subbuteo in 1947, some nine years before I was born. I am not claiming, in any shape or form, that he was the first person to bring about the concept of table football. Of course he was not. He did, however, invent, conceive, originate, devise – whichever word you think is appropriate – the phenomenon known to everyone worldwide as Subbuteo, a name synonymous with a specific genre of table top football.

It had been Dad's intention to write his own very personal experiences of his life with Subbuteo, which he liked to call his "memoirs" rather than commit himself to the rather formidable intention of "writing a book". It is his collection of photos, handwritten notes, press cuttings, which he intended to use for his writing but which sadly he never got round to, which now sits in front of me in a plain buff-coloured folder with the word 'Memoirs' written on the front in his own highly distinctive handwriting. I am now using it as the basis and inspiration for this book. Over the years, many of Dad's friends and acquaintances had told him that he should put his experiences down in writing, but the reply was always along the lines of "Who would be really interested?" Since his death in 1994, I have found out that the answer to that question is emphatic: many, many people across the world who have had Subbuteo in their lives, and still have to this day, are interested.

A few years ago, I had a sitting with a clairvoyant who told me, among other things, that she felt very strongly that I had a book in me waiting to come out, and that, on the back of this book, a lot of foreign travel would be involved. I have to say that I am not totally cynical about clairvoyance and suchlike, but it is not beyond the realms of possibility that everyone has the capacity to write a book about something, so when the book in me was touched upon, I took it to be too much of a generalisation. I wondered what on earth my book could possibly be about, and promptly dismissed the notion altogether. It was only a few years later, when I started to get phone calls from complete strangers wanting information for Subbuteo websites, and collectors of Subbuteo needing my opinion of the value of certain rare teams and accessories, that I realised that interest in Subbuteo was still as strong as it ever was. I have even received a phone call at well past midnight from a gentleman from Middlesbrough informing me that he had recently purchased an old Subbuteo set at a car-boot sale for fifty pence, and did I happen to know what the true value might be? I am always happy to try to help in these situations, but being disturbed at that ungodly hour was really a bit much! I politely informed him that without actually seeing the set in question it was rather difficult to give a valuation, but assured him that at fifty pence he had, without doubt, bought an absolute bargain. So it was that I decided it might be a good idea to write a book, from my own very unique perspective, about Subbuteo and my father, and give a glimpse of what life was like 'behind the scenes' of the world's best-known and much-loved table football game.

From the moment I realised it was my duty, and indeed honour, to write this book, I decided from the outset to give an accurate account, and not to write it through rose-tinted spectacles, not to soften any hard edges. I am sure that you, the reader, would not wish that. You want to hear it straight. And you will, I promise you.

A common assumption, voiced by numerous people over the years, is that it must have been an idealistic period for me as a youngster, and indeed for my parents, to have been surrounded and totally involved in the whole Subbuteo thing. This was not necessarily the case. Yes, there was an abundance of money around, but money does not guarantee that everything is rosy. This is real life after all. There was a lot going on under the surface that was not apparent to the casual observer. In hindsight, I am surprised that I turned out to be the reasonably normal and well-balanced individual that I am, although some may refute that statement! Of course, the good times counterbalanced the not so good, and I saw and did many things as a young boy which, were it not for Subbuteo and the lifestyle it generated, I would not have experienced. For that I owe my dad a huge debt of gratitude.

At this stage of an introduction I should tell the story of how the name Subbuteo came about. It is a question that is constantly asked of me, and rightly so, as it is quite an unusual name. The question of its origin has been raised a few times on various television and radio programmes, once on the panel game 'QI', hosted by the comedian, author and all-round sharp wit Stephen Fry, and also on Radio 2 with Steve Wright in a section he likes to call Factoids. I also recall a few newspaper articles and trivia books alluding to the origins of this extraordinary word, but I have to say, and I admit to being extremely petty here, the pronunciation always seems to rub me up the wrong way.

In the main, most people tend to pronounce the word 'Subooteo' and not 'Subewteo' which is the correct way. A small point I admit, but it never fails to annoy me.

Anyhow, the origin of the name. When Dad conceived the idea of the game he wanted to call it 'The Hobby', as in a pastime, but on approaching various patent agents and offices he was told that the name was too descriptive and too generic to be patented; that if he wanted to protect his idea he had better go away and think of another name and resubmit it. He became very frustrated by this and spent many a sleepless night mulling over another name for his brainchild. And even if he did come up with one, would the powers that be at the patent office allow him to use it? Would he be refused for a second time?

Ornithology, or birds and birdwatching to the uninitiated (the feathered variety I might add, although the skirted variety did also feature quite prominently at times, but more of that later), was of great interest to Dad, and it struck him that he could still use the word 'hobby', but in terms of the hobby hawk bird of prey. If he could perhaps find the Latin name for this particular creature, it might present a viable alternative but still keep the original idea. Scouring through the numerous bird books he owned he eventually found the hobby hawk with the Latin name of *falco subbuteo*. There it was in front of him. The answer to his dilemma. His new game was to be called Subbuteo.

Mark Adolph

Chapter 1

The Early Years

PETER ARTHUR ADOLPH, my dad, was born on 7th December 1916 in Brighton, East Sussex. At 77 Montpelier Road, Brighton, to be precise, which was, and still is to this day, a rather unremarkable street of Victorian houses, running from the seafront uphill to what is today the main shopping area of Brighton in Western Road. He was the only child of Gladys and Arthur Adolph, his father being an army officer who later became the secretary of the British Medical Association and then later on Appeals Secretary at St Bartholomew's Hospital. So he was born into an ordinary middle-class family with, for the first ten years of his life, holidays being taken on the Isle of Wight at the same time every summer without fail.

Life for the young Peter was very much on an even keel, until 1930 when his father suddenly died at the age of fifty-two from tuberculosis. Peter was only fourteen years of age. Obviously, this affected him and his mother in a bad way and almost immediately his mother decided that in both their interests, to help them get over the premature death of a much loved husband and father, they should move away from the south coast which had been their family home for a good many years, to start a new life in the London suburb of Chiswick. This was where Gladys had been brought up as a child so it seemed a logical place to relocate. She knew the area and Peter was young and would adapt easily and make new friends, as most youngsters of that age tend to do. The only worry for Gladys was that Peter, as well as herself of course, had to cope with mourning their husband and father, as well as settling into new surroundings.

They moved into what was then a relatively new semi-detached residence, in Abinger Road, Chiswick. Again, a very middle-class area of outer London. Peter was offered a place at Gunnersbury Roman Catholic Grammar School, a stone's throw from his new home in Chiswick, and it was at this school that Peter really started to flourish. He found he had a natural aptitude for figures, mental arithmetic in particular, a flair which had hitherto been dormant. It was this complete understanding of numbers and figures which would hold him in good stead in the future.

I can well remember as a young child, maybe eight or nine years old, watching Dad add up page upon page of columns of figures in his head, running his finger swiftly up and down the columns and coming up with the total at the end, and this was in the days of pounds, shillings and pence or LSD as some people used to call it. As well as using this for purely practical business purposes, it soon developed into a kind of party trick. He would be given a list of figures, not necessarily monetary figures, and he would add them up in his head while somebody else used the more conventional method of an adding machine (not a calculator in those days) and nine times out of ten he would beat them to the answer and be correct as well. I have to add this is not a skill I have inherited.

Apart from the arithmetic Peter was academically quite average, with school reports stating on more than one occasion that he had this tendency to drift off into his own little world and be completely oblivious to what was happening around him. He also found that he was developing an interest in natural history, particularly ornithology. I suppose Chiswick was not the ideal place in which to be living if this interest was to blossom, but Peter read books on the subject and soon became quite proficient at recognising various types of birds and some of their Latin names. Little did he know at the time how useful, and of course life changing, this would be in the future.

Again, attending Gunnersbury Grammar School brought out the sporting side of Peter which he hadn't realised existed. Perhaps it was a case of getting involved in some physical exercise to help him cope with the sudden change of circumstances and the loss of his father. Whatever it was that made Peter involve himself so passionately in sport seemed to work because before long he was playing cricket and football for the school team. He became so keen and proficient at cricket, bowling being his strong point, that he had a trial for Middlesex schoolboys, playing for them on a regular basis. During the winter he played football for the school, and he was picked out as a player of some potential by scouts from Brentford Football Club. Peter was offered a trial with Brentford and duly accepted. He played a couple of games for the reserves, but unfortunately failed to meet the required standard to be offered a schoolboy contract. Things could have turned out very differently had he impressed during his short spell with the west London club.

It was at Gunnersbury that Peter had a friend by the name of Geoffrey Wirrick. He lived a few streets away and was a keen football supporter, But Geoffrey followed the other west London side near to both their homes, namely Queens Park Rangers. Geoffrey, knowing that Peter had just been rejected by Brentford, played on his obvious bitterness and coaxed and cajoled him to go with him to watch their nearest rivals play. Peter and Geoffrey cycled the two miles or so from their homes in Chiswick every Saturday to watch Queens Park Rangers at Shepherds Bush. For Peter this was the start of a long-term love affair with QPR, which was passed down through the generations, to me and, in turn, to my own son, Thomas. Dad had often said that if he had to support a team other than QPR, it would have been Brentford, despite his rejection as a potential young player with the club.

Peter was now sixteen years old, and his mother was finding it extremely hard financially to look after them both. So Peter was forced to leave Gunnersbury Grammar School, with hardly any qualifications, to try and find a job to help support himself and his mother. He didn't know at all what kind of work he was suited to, but a friend of his mother's, knowing the situation and being aware of his flair for figures, managed to secure him a position as an accounts clerk at a firm called Vesty Brothers in London, a processed meat production company. Peter seemed to settle in well to his first job, thriving on the responsibility. It must also have given him a sense of being the man of the house, which I suppose quite literally he was, as he was the main breadwinner. After paying for all his and his mother's domestic bills, Peter found he still had a small amount of disposable income to indulge in a newly found interest in music.

He was a particular fan of Bing Crosby and had a fondness for the big band sound of the era. He could often be found after a day's work scouring the record stalls in Shepherds Bush market for recordings of Joe Loss and his Orchestra, Sydney Hilton, Jack Payne and his Band, and, of course, Bing Crosby, or just Bing as he affectionately called him. He would spend all evening listening to them on his 'gramophone' or tuning in to a live recording of a big band on his crystal radio set.

Such was his interest in music that by the time he was twenty-one, he joined a big band purely on an amateur basis, as a singer, or 'crooner' as they were referred to in those days. The band was The Oscar Rabin Band, or Oscar Rabin and his Romany Band as they were more commonly known. They used to perform on a regular basis at the Hammersmith Palais, at tea dances or evening concerts, and Peter's crooning experience culminated in a live broadcast from the Palais on 15th March 1939, when he sang tunes such as 'Tears On My Pillow', 'If You Were The Only Girl', 'Jeepers Creepers', and about half a dozen others. He was just twenty-two years old. I am sure that many people tuned in to listen to this broadcast on their crystal radio sets, just as Peter had been doing only a year or so earlier. If you scour through specialist record shops now it is still possible to buy recordings of Oscar Rabin and his Band, but whether they are ones with Dad singing on them, I really do not know.

Peter was a highly thought of member of staff at Vesty Brothers, so he was given the opportunity, by way of future promotion, to study Cost and Works accountancy and Spanish. The firm's beef cattle were reared in Uruguay and it was hoped that Peter would get his qualification and learn a smattering of Spanish, enough to get by initially, and go to Uruguay to work.

This never materialised as, having joined the RAF Volunteer Reserve in 1937, he was called up at the start of the Second World War in 1939, and posted to RAF Brize Norton in Oxfordshire. I think Peter was quite keen on working in South America at the time, so to have that hope dashed and be drafted to Oxfordshire to serve his country was a little annoying for him to say the least.

Family stories have it that Peter hated flying so a posting to Brize Norton was not the most appropriate place to be doing his national service, but I know this is not the case. I don't believe he would have joined the RAF Reserve in the first place had he had a fear of flying. It would not have been an option.

As it turned out, he never took to the skies and spent his time at Brize Norton driving supplies around the base and working in the stores. Not the most glamorous of jobs but someone had to do it. It was here that he learned to drive, on the RAF trucks, and he never passed a driving test.

Peter was one never to take being told what to do lightly and detested any kind of authority figure. He was very much his own person. One day he was told by a very senior officer to get his hair cut. Peter, being Peter, turned round and in no uncertain terms told him to "get your own bloody hair cut"! Subsequently, he spent the next seven days in "jankers" as he called it. Jail to you and me. He never regretted his outburst and insisted he would say it again if he had to, and suffer the consequences once more. That's how he was.

I remember him telling me that after the war, whenever he was trying to impress the ladies, he would tell them that he served in the RAF for the duration of the war, which, of course, was quite correct. But instead of telling them what he really did, he said unashamedly that he, and I quote his exact words here, "was a navigator in a bomber over Berlin". He even used this line on my mother when they first met, but I think she saw through his little lies! It became a bit of a family 'in joke', and because he worked in the stores I used to call him "a potato peeler".

When the war finished Peter was returned to civilian life, none the worse for wear after his rather cushy spell at Brize Norton. Near the end of the war his mother had moved from Chiswick to the little Kentish village of Langton Green which is located a couple of miles from Tunbridge Wells. It was to this new home that Peter returned. The house was called

The Lodge, a single-storey building standing at the intersection of a main road and an extremely long driveway which led to a large private house called Ashurst Place, now used as a private nursing home. Their new home, as the name implies, used to be the lodge or gatehouse for this very dominating building in the mid-1800s.

1946 was a hard time for a lot of people. Many men were finding it difficult to get back onto a pre-war footing and find their way in a much-changing Britain. Peter, of course, was no different and the future was looking a little bleak for him. No job and year upon year of not much to look forward to, or so it appeared. Peter never had been one to rest on his laurels, so with much determination and resolve he decided to use his pre-war knowledge of figures and accounts and bookkeeping to land himself a job in London as a civil servant with the Pensions Office.

This meant many hours travelling from Tunbridge Wells to London, and I don't think that the irony was lost on him that, had he still been living in Chiswick, it would have made his life a lot easier. But he was living in the Garden of England, and at least he had a job with reasonable, if not fantastic, pay.

But Peter very quickly started to get extremely bored with office life, and his enthusiasm for the job soon waned. He had started paying too much attention to the female workers and on more than one occasion had to be cautioned by his superiors for sitting around the typing pool with the secretaries, not doing a stroke of work. Another brush with authority was very much on the cards. One final caution by his bosses was too much for Peter and he told them what they could with his job and promptly left. No jankers this time, but he was out of a job and had to get himself back on track pretty quickly.

It was now that the real entrepreneurial side of Peter really started to take hold, and so he grabbed the bull by the horns and decided that working for someone else was not for him. The only way forward in this life was to work for yourself, to be in control of your own destiny without someone constantly looking over your shoulder and telling you what you should and should not be doing. He decided that he would start his own natural history business from scratch, dealing mainly in rare birds' eggs. He had a few contacts which he had made over the years from his general interest in the subject and it was now time to put these to good use. He soon found that there were many like-minded people around who shared his interest in natural history and ornithology in particular, and his business started to take off. But he very quickly realised that due to Mother Nature this was a very seasonal business. The spring and summer months were very good and he made money during these times, but as soon as autumn and winter took hold, business completely dried up and he was left wondering where the next penny would be coming from. What to do? He needed to be earning some money during the winter.

What Peter did not want was to work for someone else again. He was definitely cut out to be his own boss, not to pander to others. With the upsurge of interest in sports after the war, especially in football and to a lesser extent cricket, and on a complete whim, Peter thought that it would be a good idea to see if it was feasible to make a football game that could be played by all the family, especially during long winter months. After all, as with the natural history business, he would be turning an interest into something he could possibly make money from.

Peter was aware there had been a table-top football game on the market before the war called Newfooty, but this had ceased production with the onset of hostilities although, confusingly, there were some people who say that the game carried on in production right through the war and never stopped until the early sixties. It is a debate which will continue for a very long time, I am sure, but Peter thought that he could improve on any football game on the market and it was when he was whiling away a few empty hours at home at The Lodge that he started fiddling around with an old blue button that had come off his mother's coat. It suddenly dawned on him that what he had in his hand could be the breakthrough he was looking for in his football game. The button had a flat bottom and rounded sides, but was hollow in the middle. He thought that if a washer or another type of weight was placed in this space it would give the base balance and swerve. He tested his theory and found it worked. It was a definite improvement on many of the other football games around.

Peter thought he was on to something, but decided to test the market, without any product being available, before continuing any further down the line. So he placed an advert in *Boy's*

Own magazine which had a circulation of around 250,000. He had no real idea of how the game would eventually be presented, if at all, but more or less plucked a selling price out of thin air. It would cost seven shillings and sixpence (37.5p). The advertisement cost him the princely sum of two pounds and ten shillings (£2.50).

He applied for a patent and registered the game. Interestingly, no mention was made in the patent of the now famous flicking method of propulsion, or fingertip control. Instead, it stated that propulsion was by means of using an implement similar to the small, flat wooden spoons that were used when eating from an ice-cream tub. It just goes to show how embryonic the idea was, and that it was still fermenting inside Peter's head. The advert was due to appear in the *Boy's Own* in the late summer of 1946 and Peter had done all he could for the time being. The only thing to do was sit back and see if he got any response from his shot-in-the-dark advert.

Meanwhile, he was to concentrate on his natural history business and out of the blue he got a call from an egg collector in America asking him if he was able to evaluate his collection. This was in the days when this type of collecting was perfectly legal, not frowned upon at all. Peter jumped at a trip to the USA. It would mean a boost to his business. He promptly booked himself on the first available trip on the RMS *Queen Elizabeth* sailing to New York. Although he was focused on his upcoming collection evaluation, aboard the *Queen Elizabeth* he still found his mind wandering to the advertisement and how he would proceed further if, hope of hopes, something should come of it. If it did, it would only be a few general enquires he thought, but he felt he had to be at least mentally prepared for any possible outcome.

It was on the second day of his stay in New York that Peter, preparing himself for that afternoon's visit to his American client, heard a knock on the door of his hotel room. It was the bellboy from the hotel reception, standing there with a cable in his hand which he passed to Peter. He tipped him and sat on the bed to read the cable. Could it be from his client cancelling the appointment? Had he made the long trip to the USA for nothing? Although he had certainly experienced an interesting and very enjoyable journey on the certainly if nothing else. On closer inspection he noticed the cable was from England. Something is wrong with Mum, he must have thought. Indeed, the cable was from his mother, but it informed him that she had received a total of £7,500 in 7s.6d postal orders in response to his advert in *Boy's Own*, each one ordering a game which did not exist. In Peter's mind it did, certainly, but there was nothing of a tangible nature. His mother also wanted to know what she should do with the postal orders. Peter cabled back immediately with the response: "Bank them." These days such an amount would be worth more than £200,000.

Peter kept his appointment that afternoon and, with his mind still racing, tried to evaluate his client's egg collection as best he could under the circumstances. He had planned to stay in New York for a while to take in the sights of this magnificent city, but such was his eagerness to return to England as soon as possible, he cut short his trip. He could always come back another time, maybe even as a rich man.

Back home in Langton Green, Peter's mother was frantically doing all she could to prepare for her son's imminent return, and the production and despatch of his new football game, although without him actually being there to oversee proceedings her help would be somewhat limited.

She did manage, however, to enlist the help of a close friend of Peter's, Jim Murphy, who lived in Tunbridge Wells. Everyone called him Spud for some reason, probably a cross between the Irish surname and the Irish Potato Famine of 1845. In later years he was just plain old 'Uncle Spud' to me. Having had the situation about her son's activities explained to him, although I think he already knew about the advert, Spud was very sceptical about whether they could actually produce and despatch a game in a reasonable amount of time to those who had parted with their hard-earned cash. With a great deal of persuasion and positive talking she managed to win Spud round and by the time Peter had arrived back from his trip to the USA, the orders had been systematically filed and the postal orders counted and banked, ready for the important part of the operation – producing a football game.

They had turned an unused spare bedroom at the rear of the house into something resembling a command centre, from where all the games were to be produced, assembled and despatched. The main problem was the post-war lack of raw materials, so they had to make the best of what was available at the time. Having the bases moulded would have been a very time-consuming process under the circumstances, so Peter decided that his best bet would be to revert to his original idea of using buttons. He made a bulk purchase of plastic buttons from Woolworth's, similar to the one from his mother's coat, which would then be cut to shape and lead washers used to add ballast and balance.

Wire goals with paper nets were made and acetate balls were sourced quite quickly. There was to be no pitch for these early games, instead a packet of chalk was included in the sets with the suggestion that the pitch be marked out on an old army blanket. What Peter did not anticipate was that this did actually prove to be very popular with customers as they could determine their own size of playing pitch, which meant playing on a table was easier than having a regular-sized pitch which was likely to mean playing on the floor. The texture of the army blanket was also ideally suited for playing the game as it gave purchase when flicking the figures. There was no research done into the army blanket: it was just plain good luck that it happened to be so perfect. And in those days most households had one.

The cardboard playing figures which were to sit on top of the bases proved a sticking point – no pun intended. There was no quick method of having these produced. A great deal of searching led to a firm in Leeds by the name of Petty and Company who were able to print the figures in the fastest possible time.

They were to be printed in basic red shirt, white shorts and blue shirt format. These were the quickest and cheapest colours to print at the time and by now every second counted.

Peter, his mother and Spud spent every available hour cutting bases, assembling goals, but they were still awaiting the arrival of the elusive printed figures from Petty and Co. which were taking longer than expected. By the early part of 1947 Peter was receiving letters from customers who had paid their money only to find no game was forthcoming. A few people even accused Peter of being a conman such was the delay in fulfilling the orders in a reasonable amount of time. To this end Peter placed another advert in the magazine, apologising profusely for the delay in the despatch of the games, explaining that a delay in manufacturing was to blame and orders would be sent out as soon as possible.

This appeared to appease the anxious customers, the letters of complaint died down considerably and all three of them were able to tackle the task in hand. The printed figures had arrived and they all breathed a sigh of relief for they could now finalise the orders, assemble the boxes and despatch the games to their rightful owners.

This had taken around six months from the time of the first *Boy's Own* advert. A new patent had been applied for, and subsequently granted, incorporating the fingertip control method rather than the 'spoons' idea.

I believe that having capital in the bank from advance orders on a product that had yet to be produced is a unique situation for any new enterprise. All the while further orders for the game had been flooding in on the back of the original advert, but at least now the original ones had been dealt with and something resembling a system had now developed, making the processing of the subsequent orders a lot easier to handle.

Peter was by now in a buoyant mood over the initial response to his game, and he sent a note, together with advertising leaflets, to a good friend of his in ornithological circles. It was handwritten on headed notepaper which had printed on the top, P.A. ADOLPH, DISTRIBUTOR OF "TABLE SOCCER" (patent applied for). The note read as follows:

To. Major W. M. Congreve
You may be interested to see
What I have been doing in my spare
Time (between 3&4 am in the morning!)
p.a.a. 11/3/47
Somehow I think my "boys" will go
For it as a winter occupation. Has CHG
Still his magazine going?

Not one to let a situation rest, Peter decided to advertise again in *Boy's Own* magazine, and the *Eagle* comic, and presumably he was after some information from his friend Major Congreve about other magazines in which to advertise. Once again the response was overwhelming with many thousands of customers sending in their money for this new table football game. The game was becoming self-capitalising because it was only available by mail-order.

Until 1948 all leaflets and adverts simply had the words "It's a Sports Game" printed on them as a basic description, but Peter wanted to create a more substantial identity for his new game and applied to register the trademark as 'The Hobby'. As we know, this was thought of as too generic and a now famous and recognisable name was born, one which would be associated with a specific type of table football all over the world.

It was now that Peter tried some very underhand tactics. The rival Newfooty game had been using endorsements by Stanley Matthews, so without hesitation Peter set about getting printed thousands of leaflets for Subbuteo stating that Stanley Matthews also endorsed his new game. Of course, he had no permission from the great man himself. Peter spent a fortune on these leaflets, knowing full well there might be some comeback, either from Newfooty or more likely from Matthews. He was chancing his arm here and not surprisingly it was well and truly bitten. He received a letter from Stanley Matthews personally stating in no uncertain terms that if Peter did not destroy these leaflets straight away he would sue him up to the eyeballs. Peter, of course, did not have a leg to stand on and grudgingly withdrew the leaflets, burning every one of them. All that money up in smoke, but it was certainly cheaper and less hassle than being taken to court. I think Peter learned his lesson on this occasion.

It soon became very apparent that the spare back

bedroom at The Lodge was just not able to cope with the influx of orders. The lack of space was starting to have an effect on the system used to deal with orders. More space was definitely required so Peter started making enquires about a property in the centre of Langton Green which had suitable outbuildings. The cherry on the cake as far as this potential property was concerned was that it was right next door to the village post office, which would be beneficial as far as mail-order was concerned.

He viewed other properties in the area but none were as suitable as the one in the village centre. So Peter decided to go for the property which was called Upper Birchetts. It was a three-storey building, large enough for him and his mother to live in. To the rear was a double garage with enormous storage rooms above. It had been a stable and a hayloft many years previously.

Having moved in, Peter found he had too much space at that time. He soon realised he had to justify the financial outlay on the new premises, that each square foot had to be paying its way.

The cut-down buttons were soon to be a thing of the past and the bases were now to be moulded in Maidstone, Kent, giving the game a much more professional feel, both visually and when playingit. Toy shops and sports shops were being targeted by Peter as potential retail outlets for the game, but for some strange reason, at that moment anyway, none of the shops were remotely interested in taking Subbuteo. Peter tried to get them interested in a sale or return scheme, but again no one was interested. So the business was forced to keep operating on a mail-order basis only for the time being.

Peter had by now been receiving many letters from customers wanting to know if they were able to purchase teams in their favourite club colours, instead of playing with the red and blue shirted figures and just using their imagination. Of course, this was to be the way forward. Purchasing their first set would be just the start of their involvement with the game and they would want to collect more teams and accessories. Peter could see straight away that this was more or less a licence to print money. First, get them hooked and then reel them in was how he used to describe this. Mercenary for sure, but business is business!

Buoyed on by this early success, Peter thought it would be beneficial to take his game to a toys and games convention in Brussels, Belgium, to see what response the Europeans would have to it, and also to find out the logistics of expanding the game into mainland Europe. On his arrival in Belgium, it suddenly occurred to him that, of course, he would have to present the game in French, of which he had just a smattering. For some reason, it never entered his head that this would be the case. He thought that everyone would understand it in English. A typically English attitude! However, French it had to be and so to give himself a little courage he started to hit the complimentary alcohol a little too vigorously. He managed to present his game to the convention – just – but later on had to be carried back to his hotel room to sleep it off.

When he returned to Langton Green after the convention a letter was waiting for him from a Belgian solicitor. It stated that Peter had paid far too much attention to the wife of one of the delegates, while being the worse for wear following his alcohol consumption, and that this particular man would be challenging him to a dual with swords! Peter took legal advice on the matter and agreed to pay the offended delegate a sum that would satisfy his dignity. A sum he later agreed would have satisfied anyone's dignity!

The Subbuteo machine was now on a roll and to celebrate he went out and treated himself to a brand-new car – a Bristol 400 series (OPJ 6); the first of three Bristol cars he would own.

Chapter 2

When Peter Met Pam

THE HAPPY COUPLE stand on the steps of Saint Peter's Church, Brighton, East Sussex. She is twenty-four and he is thirty-seven. She looks in every way like a model of the time, the fifties. A biased opinion it may be, but in my eyes it is true. Her wedding dress is calf length in navy blue, not the traditional white because, I was told when I was old enough to understand, she would have felt a hypocrite wearing the traditional colour of chastity and virtue. A bold and daring statement on the biggest day of her life so far. He stands next to her holding her hand tightly. He is a slender man with a pronounced receding hairline, looking slightly uneasy at the attention of the photographer and the onlooking guests. A shy and reserved man in such situations, but this shyness certainly took a back seat when it came to the cut and thrust of business.

This wedding photo of Mum and Dad, Peter Adolph and Pamela Whelan, taken on 17th July 1954, is certainly one of my favourites and one which I cherish. On Peter's right stands his best man, Jim 'Spud' Murphy, his close friend and business colleague in his new and ever-growing venture. My grandmother, Gladys, Peter's mother, stands next to her only child with a face like thunder which was totally in character. For although she departed this life when I was only five years old, I can only remember her as the archetypal old battleaxe. For some reason she seemed to despise my mother, presumably because she was the one who took her little boy away from the family home at the ripe old age of thirty-seven together with his dog, a Cairn terrier who answered to the name of Badger. My grandparents on my mother's side, however, appear in the photo as all self-respecting parents should be on their daughter's wedding day. They are the epitome of happiness, especially my granddad Dave, who only a few years previously, did not approve of his daughter's relationship with this man from Tunbridge Wells on the grounds that he was thirteen years her senior and that he had never met him.

Pam had not spoken too much about Peter to her father as she knew what his reaction would be. But his attitude to this Peter Adolph changed completely one evening when Peter came to collect Pam from their flat and family home in Grand Parade, Brighton. A car horn sounded outside in the road so Pam was escorted down the stairs to the front door by her father, who I suppose wanted to catch a glimpse of the man who was taking her out. What sort of vehicle would he be driving? By the sound of the horn it certainly was not a bicycle, probably some run of the mill Austin or Wolseley. What he saw took him back somewhat, for there parked outside his home, its two-litre engine idling with a menacing, deep throated growl was a new 400 series Bristol.

From that day forward a mutual respect between Peter and Dave was formed and eventually it became quite a close friendship which was just as well as they were soon to be related. Not long after the revelation of the Bristol, Pam came home from another date with Peter and mentioned to her father, as if trying to cement his recent change of attitude towards him, that on paying for their restaurant bill that evening Peter had produced from his pocket, and these were her words not mine, a wad of notes large enough "to choke a horse". I'd not heard that expression before and never have since, but it seems to paint the picture very accurately. What did this man from Tunbridge Wells do for a living? Where did all the cash and fast cars come from? Dave had not got a clue and I am sure Pam was not one hundred per cent sure either despite numerous dates with Peter. He seemed to keep it under his hat for some reason, but the truth will out eventually.

Peter had met Pam during one of his many visits to the pubs and dance halls in Brighton. He did not have as much leisure time as he would have liked, as he was totally involved in his new business venture, but when he did, he liked to spend it in Brighton. I suppose being born and brought up in the town, he had laid down strong roots and anyway Brighton was a more happening place than Tunbridge Wells. It still is to this very day. It also gave him the opportunity to give his pride and joy, the Bristol 400, a good run down to the coast and stretch its legs a bit.

This was a race-bred car and needed to be driven as such, which Peter certainly did whenever the opportunity arose. Another reason for visiting Brighton was that he had a girlfriend in Brighton, a girl called Cherry, and it was when he was at a dance hall in Brighton with Cherry that he met Pam. I think Pam totally knocked him off his feet when he first clapped eyes on her. I know that sounds extremely corny but I believe that is what happened. Without telling Cherry, he arranged a date with Pam for the following week. They met up, and the rest as they say is history.

Pam was born in Tottenham, north London, but having moved all over the country during the war, finally settled in Brighton with her parents and younger brother, David where she worked as a receptionist and typist at a local building firm.

By 1951 Peter and Pam were very much an item and had been going out together for about two years. Pam eventually found out what Peter's business was and despite not being all that impressed by the seemingly bottomless pit of money was very happy to go away with him on various trips abroad. Some were on business and some for pleasure. Sometimes both, if he could get away with it as far as the tax man was concerned. It soon became very apparent that Peter and Pam were in it for the long haul, and in May 1952 they became engaged.

Pam's parents were thrilled that their daughter would be marrying this charming man from Tunbridge Wells, and I would think that the trappings of a successful businessman made Peter seem that little bit more charming. He seemed to get on really well with Pam's family, which was good news despite the rather hesitant start.

Back in Langton Green, Peter's mother was still

working all the hours God sent fulfilling the orders that were still pouring in. Peter was as well, but he had to juggle his time between Pam in Brighton and Subbuteo in Langton: the two loves of his life. Pam was very understanding as she realised that it was this 'other woman' – and I am sure it must have felt like that at times – that was giving her the lifestyle to which she was becoming accustomed.

The sooner they were married the better, she thought. She and Peter had already had lengthy discussions as to where they would live after they were married and it seemed only logical that she should move from Brighton to the Tunbridge Wells area where the business was situated. The only problem was where. Peter ideally wanted to live as close to the business as possible without having to start married life living with his mother. And I am sure that no newly married woman would want to start out living with her mother-in-law. Peter kept his eyes open for any property that became available for sale within easy walking distance of Upper Birchetts, but nothing did.

It was while walking Badger around the village one Sunday afternoon that he noticed that a large field right opposite his current home was unexpectedly up for sale. Peter had not noticed the 'For Sale' sign before so he assumed that it must have just been put up. First thing Monday morning he made enquires about the land and was told that the plot was approximately six acres. He knew the land well, but he had no idea it was that large. The proximity to his business was just what he was looking for and after a quick consultation with Pam over the phone decided there and then to buy it and have his own architect-designed house built on it. He swiftly engaged the services of a local architect by the name of Philip Beecham and between them they got their heads together to design the perfect home for himself and his soon-to-be wife.

Meanwhile, the order processing for Subbuteo was starting to get behind and Peter began getting letters from customers enquiring about the whereabouts of the game they had ordered. Not quite on the scale as he had with the original orders, but complaints nevertheless and just when things were beginning to run smoothly as well. This was not what Peter wanted and it felt as if he was taking a step backwards. It was time to rethink his strategy because his mother was on the point of giving up her entirely unpaid work and going on strike.

Advertising in the local press, he quickly hired the help, paid of course, of two local men, George Underwood and Ron Reader. The former had served in the Royal Navy during the war and had a similar mind to Peter's. He had always been interested in the toys and games industry. Although he had never worked in it, he had devised a few games in his head. George was also a very keen and able golfer, playing off a very low handicap. He tried very hard to get Peter interested in the game, but failed miserably. Peter always maintained that golf just spoiled a good walk. To be honest, Ron's background was unknown when he joined Peter's expanding empire, but he lived only down the road, which under the circumstances was as good a reason as any to bring him on board. Both men were delighted to be recruited into this young and upcoming business, which by now was starting to be noticed in the local area. These two men were to be Peter's loyal and very able lieutenants for the next twenty years or so.

With this newly recruited workforce, his mother was now able to take more of a back seat which I am sure she was not too unhappy about. Despite this, she could often be found sticking her oar in where it was not entirely wanted, telling George and Ron, and sometimes even her own son, what should and should not be done. I am sure she meant well, but it was now time for her to realise that she would be playing a more passive role in her son's business.

The assembly and despatch of the games were now running smoothly again, thanks to the new recruits and the outbuildings behind the house were being utilised to their full capacity. The original cardboard playing figures had been replaced by flat celluloid figures that were already stamped out for assembly, although Peter had decided to keep the cardboard figures going for a little while longer to give the customer a choice of figure construction.

The plans for the new house were nearly completed and the building work was ready to start at any moment. Peter and Pam were starting to see their new home taking shape although it was highly unlikely that it would be ready for them to move in just after they were married. That meant living with Peter's mother at Upper Birchetts for a short time. The wedding day had been arranged for Saturday

17th July 1954 in about six months' time and Peter and Pam, together with her parents, were making the necessary arrangements for the big day. Peter's mother on the other hand appeared to be doing very little to make her son's big day one to remember. She seemed a very bitter old woman.

By now, Peter had sold his Bristol 400 and had replaced it with the latest model, a 401 series (UML 548), which he had bought from University Motors in Piccadilly, exclusive agents for Bristol Cars Ltd. It created a lot of attention wherever he drove it, not least with his future father-in-law and Pam's brother David. Peter was certainly going up in the world, and with his newly earned money was able to indulge his rather expensive passions.

The next six months appeared to fly by and everything was now in place for Peter and Pam's wedding day. The day arrived and by three o'clock in the afternoon the new Mr and Mrs Adolph appeared in front of the main door of Saint Peter's Church, Brighton, to the frenzied click of camera shutters from friends and family with the official photos being taken by a Langton Green resident, a professional photographer and good friend of Peter's named Michael Wheeler, who would soon become involved in Subbuteo in quite a big way, taking shots for most of its promotional literature and advertising campaigns. His wife June was to become one of Pam's best friends and she was to become godmother to one of their children, Clare. So quite a bond was formed between the Adolphs and the Wheelers over the years. After the reception at the Ship Hotel in

Brighton, Peter and Pam set off for their honeymoon in Italy, which was to be a driving holiday in Peter's new Bristol 401.

It was while on their honeymoon in Italy that Peter realised how far Subbuteo had come in the consciousness of the general public in a short space of time and it quite took him aback for a while. They were staying at a beautiful hotel on Lake Maggiore in northern Italy, about a hundred miles north of Milan, practically on the Swiss border. It was an idyllic place in which to spend a honeymoon – mountains, lakes and plenty of sunshine. Just what they both needed after months of planning the wedding, trying to get a new home built and, of course, the day-to-day running of Subbuteo. They had just finished dinner one evening in the hotel restaurant, and had ventured into the bar for a coffee and nightcap, when they struck up a conversation with an English couple in their mid-to-late sixties. They came from Cheshire and were spending a lot of their retirement years travelling around Europe. In the course of general conversation Peter was asked what he did for a living and he told them that he had only recently started his own company, not thinking to mention it was Subbuteo because he really did not imagine that anyone would have heard of it. The name did not matter he thought. When pushed for further information, the Subbuteo word was mentioned and to Peter's delight, and I suppose shock, the couple from Cheshire had actually heard of Subbuteo because they had recently ordered a game for their grandson's upcoming birthday. Peter laughed and promised that when he returned to England he would check out the order and give it priority despatch status so that their grandson would receive it in good time. The couple were duly impressed with this form of hands-on customer relations and Peter kept his word. He later received a letter from the couple saying that the game was received well on time and thanked him for his help. This was most certainly one way of attracting brand loyalty and one which would hopefully generate future orders.

This encounter was to be the first of many business related transactions that would be had by Peter in the relaxed and congenial surroundings of a pub, club or restaurant. He would never be the type of employer to call a formal meeting of his colleagues and staff to discuss business in a boardroom or office if he could help it. A drink or a meal would produce much better results for everyone concerned. Not exactly the normal executive procedure, but Peter was not your normal businessman; he was very much his own person.

Relaxed and refreshed from their Italian honeymoon, Peter and Pam returned to Langton Green and took up temporary residence with his mother at Upper Birchetts. The house across the road was starting to take shape and Peter often took time out to walk across to see how things were progressing. I think he felt that if the builders knew he could appear at any given moment there would be no slacking on the job and the house would be completed in a reasonable time. This appeared to have the desired effect because by February 1955, despite some normal setbacks and unavoidable delays, the house was more or less ready. This coincided with Pam discovering that she was three months pregnant which was not the best of timing but they were both thrilled and Peter laid down the law, which most expectant fathers do, that she should take it easy and not do too much. Pam was starting to feel unwell almost on a daily basis and they started to be very concerned that all was not well with the pregnancy. Trips to the doctor revealed nothing untoward and she was told that it was probably just early days and not to become unduly worried. Easy to say, but not easy to do, and still Pam remained in a constant state of malaise, not being able to say exactly what was wrong, just a general feeling of being unwell and run down. It all came to an unfortunate head when she was visiting her parents in Brighton and her mother had to make a phone call to Peter saying that Pam had had a miscarriage and had lost the baby. It was a baby girl.

It goes without saying that they were both devastated by this loss, but the only thing to do was to look forward and move on as best they could. Luckily, moving into the house took their minds off their sorrow and they immersed themselves in the move. Peter had to explain the situation to George and Ron that due to Pam's miscarriage and moving into the house, he would not be able to be as hands-on as he had been for a few weeks, and that it was up to them to make sure that the good ship Subbuteo would maintain its steady course.

The house was just what they had dreamed of

except it lacked enough furniture to fill the rooms. Like anyone moving into a new home, they had to make do with some old furniture from his mother's house until they found some of their own. It wasn't lack of funds; it was that they wanted it to be just right. The house needed a name, as it was only referred to as a plot number which was not very romantic.

Choosing a suitable name for your home can be a little tricky. You do not want it to sound too pretentious or naff. There was a house on the nearby Ashdown Forest which Peter always admired when he took Badger for a walk. It was called Little Abbotts, and presumably only the owners knew the reason. But Peter always thought that was a good name to call a house. It just sounded right. Something along those lines would be ideal and between them they came up with the name Little Pryors. Spelling it with a 'Y' rather than the more normal 'I' meant double confusion as Adolph was often spelled with an 'F'. Now they had to contend with many misspellings of their house name as well.

Little Pryors was not quite as large as you might imagine considering the amount of land it occupied. It had only two bedrooms and the usual quota of reception rooms. It was only in the late sixties that it was extended, with a further bedroom, with a roof-top terrace, and a large games room underneath, with an attached double garage. The games room, or the 'big room' which we later called it, was used to house Peter's ornithological paraphernalia as well as having a permanent Subbuteo table. At one end was a sitting area with sofa and coffee table, and at the other end was a very large Zenith stereogram, a word which has now gone out of existence. The Zenith was the size of a dining-room sideboard and was a beautiful piece of furniture as well as a music machine.

Outside was a formal garden of about an acre, with a yew hedge encircling the house to make a boundary between this formal garden and the other five acres of woods and fields that lay beyond which had two commercial sized greenhouses situated at their furthest end. All this was a big step up from the relatively cramped surroundings across the road at Upper Birchetts.

Having more or less settled into their new surroundings, Peter was soon back at the helm of Subbuteo overseeing its continuing progress. Orders were still coming in at a steady rate and the games now included a green baize cloth, marked out as a standard soccer pitch, except for a shooting line. A small range of accessories were starting to become available and there was a choice of twenty-four different team strips. That does not sound a lot but it must be remembered that in those days one team strip could actually represent three or four different clubs. There was not the subtle difference in strips then as there is today.

Pam was well and truly back on her feet after the upset and trauma of the miscarriage and in early September Peter booked a surprise trip for her to the South of France to really cement her recovery. She had no idea the trip was on the cards until one day Peter came home and waved a couple of plane tickets under her nose. Not only were they plane tickets but they were first-class plane tickets. They would be flying the next day on Air France to Nice and then on to a five-star hotel in Menton, a few miles up the coast. Again, he briefed Ron and George and told them that he would phone every day to see if any problems had occurred during his absence. The two weeks that they spent in Menton were just the tonic they needed. They soaked up the early autumn French sunshine, hiring a car to do some sightseeing along the beautiful coastline of southern France, and enjoying the delights of French wine and cuisine.

During one of his daily calls, Peter was told by George that, out of the blue, several of the retail outlets he contacted previously about stocking Subbuteo sets had suddenly had a change of heart and now appeared very eager to take the product. Obviously, they had realised how well it was selling by mail-order and wanted a piece of the action. Up until that point Peter and Pam were thinking of staying on in France for another week, but with this news Peter thought it would be best to return on the date planned and deal with these retailers as soon as possible before their interest went off the boil. He could not afford to keep them waiting for an answer and it certainly would not look at all good if they knew he had decided to stay on in France for a third luxurious week.

On their return, Peter contacted the retailers, negotiating a deal with most of them to stock a number of Subbuteo games and accessories on a trial basis. One shop, George Coker Sports in Tunbridge Wells, was, as the name implies, primarily a sports accessory suppliers. It was the first time they had stocked games, albeit a sports game. The response from this particular outlet was way beyond expectations and they sold their initial quota of games over one weekend. Another order was placed and again the same thing happened. Soon they became the main stockist of Subbuteo in the Tunbridge Wells area.

Not only was the news good regarding the initial success of Subbuteo in retail establishments, more good news was to follow that Pam was pregnant again. Naturally, both Peter and Pam were thrilled with this news but their excitement was quite rightly dampened with the experience of the previous pregnancy. Caution and plenty of rest was to be the order of the day as far as Pam was concerned. Throughout the coming months Pam was checked regularly to make certain all was going as well as it should be. It was, and at Pembury hospital, near Tunbridge Wells, on Wednesday 20th June 1956 at 12.50 pm Pam gave birth to a healthy baby boy, weighing in at nine pounds. Yours truly.

As if to celebrate the birth of his new son, Peter traded in his second Bristol for his third, and final, Bristol, a 405 series. I suppose buying a four-door saloon was Peter's way of bowing to fatherhood. It was a more family-orientated car, although still an extremely powerful machine!

Chapter 3

Subbuteo grows up

AS IF THE acquisition of retail outlets and the birth of his first child were not enough, 1956 also saw a giant leap forward for Subbuteo as a company and manufacturer. By Christmas that year Subbuteo had started the very liberating process of being able to mould their own bases for the game and Dad engaged the services of the Medway Tool Company, conveniently located in the small market town of Paddock Wood, some eight miles from Tunbridge Wells, right in the heart of the hop-growing region of Kent.

The owner of The Medway Tool Company was Roy Tickle, a very jovial man who was an expert in his field. What Roy did not know about tool-making and the injection-moulding world was not really worth knowing. He and Dad struck up an immediate friendship as well as a very sound business relationship, and as usual with Dad, a lot of his business with Roy was conducted after official business hours over a few pints of beer at one of the local public houses.

By the early sixties, it became apparent that Roy was toying with the idea of selling his moulding business, and Dad, never one to miss a trick, started negotiations with the aim of buying the business and having his own moulding factory. The sale went through and the company was immediately renamed Subbuteo Limited, a subsidiary of Subbuteo Sports Games. Dad now had two businesses. Suddenly, he found that although he was in total control of all moulding output, there was a surplus of moulding machines lying idle most of the time which, of course, was not cost-effective. Dad was by now making many contacts in the toys and games industry and it was after a chance meeting with one of the top directors of a company called Lines Brothers that he saw where the immediate future for these idle machines lay. Lines Brothers produced the driving figures that sat in the Scalextric racing cars as well as the trackside accessories, and a mutually beneficial deal was negotiated whereby Subbuteo Limited would mould these figures for Lines Brothers.

Problem solved, or so Dad thought, but even then Subbuteo Limited was not working to full capacity as the Scalextric contract was not as large as first imagined. Acting again on trade contacts Dad secured more work to take up the slack and started moulding for Dinky Toys.

This was great news for a boy of about five or six years old. Not only did I receive a good number of free toy cars from Dinky Toys I also remember going over to the factory with Dad on occasions and being allowed to take home any items that did not quite come up to standard. Rejects, I suppose. Not that I noticed any faults at all: they were only conspicuous to the trained and professional eye. It was great. I vaguely remember playing some gruesome game with the Scalextric drivers as they were only moulded from the chest upwards with outstretched arms to fit on the cars. In my mind they had been horribly mutilated by some toy lion and only the top half of the body remained. Only a six-year-old boy could have an imagination like that – or was it just me?

Geoffrey Samson was appointed Sales Manager in 1961 and Sammy, as he soon became known by all at Subbuteo, brought with him a wealth of experience in his field of sales. He had previously worked for Mars in Europe during the war and it was in Belgium that he met his wife Julie. Sammy brought with him an entire sales force to Subbuteo and he conducted the sales operation from his home in Patcham, near Brighton. Sammy and Julie were to become my godparents, such was the relationship that grew with Mum and Dad.

Every Monday without fail Sammy and Julie would drive up to Langton Green from Brighton, Sammy spending all day at the Subbuteo office and Julie spending the day with Mum and me at Little Pryors. Being Belgian, Julie was very demonstrative in her affections towards me and I recall always having to brace myself to receive her hugs and kisses on arrival. I found it all a little overwhelming even at the tender age of six or seven. On occasions, Mum and I would meet Julie in the restaurant of a large department store in Tunbridge Wells named Weekes, where I was greeted by Julie in the same enthusiastic manner but this time in front of the general public. I remember dreading this public show of affection and I often asked Mum if she could have a word with Julie and tell her how embarrassing it was for me.

I suppose she meant well, and often the situation was defused somewhat by Julie buying me the most enormous Knickerbocker Glory ice-cream you can imagine. I looked forward to the ice-cream treats but never, ever the affection that preceded it. Couldn't she have just stuck to the ice-cream?

After a hard Monday at the office, Sammy and Dad would walk across the road to Little Pryors and relax with a few glasses of whisky. Julie always showed the same degree of affection towards her returning husband as she had to me earlier in the day – perhaps even a little more – but it still turned my stomach. She was a lovely lady but for some reason I had always been slightly wary of Sammy. Maybe it was his hard businessman's demeanour that I found a bit intimidating, but I think deep down he was a very kind man and I know he thought the world of me.

With Sammy firmly established as Dad's right-hand man, a major growth period for Subbuteo was now under way. Dad realised that if Subbuteo Limited was producing three-dimensional figures for Scalextric and Dinky Toys, there was no reason why it should not be producing similar three dimensional figures for the playing figures or 00 scale figures as they were to be called. These new figures were to be marketed under the 'Continental' range and were far more labour intensive to produce. Each figure had to be hand-assembled and hand-painted and this is where the now infamous Subbuteo outworkers' scheme came into operation. The moulded figures would be delivered to the workers' houses firstly to be hand-painted for which the pay would be around £1/10s for every thousand. It did not matter if it was Leeds United in their simple all white strip or a much more complicated team strip the pay was just the same. It was the luck of the draw.

Then the painted figures and bases would be packed off to another outworker for the figures to be assembled. The footballs themselves, moulded in two halves, were also assembled by outworkers, but this was only for the hardy souls who did not mind their whole house smelling of trichoethelene, or 'trike' for short. This was the chemical used to melt the two halves together as glue would just create an uneven bond and so impair the running of the ball.

It was on the outworker run during the school holidays when I was around eleven or twelve that I used to earn a bit of pocket money by helping out the delivery driver, who went by the name of Bill Olley. He was a chirpy East Ender who always wore dark glasses no matter the weather. It always seemed to amuse me, but I am easily amused, I suppose.

My job was really to help Bill load the van up with bases, painted figures, washers and glue and despatch them to the outworkers' homes. At first, the van was an unmarked white transit type of vehicle but it was very soon replaced by a van which no one could help but notice, painted entirely in Subbuteo green with the Subbuteo logo emblazoned on every available panel. All it needed was to play the 'Match of the Day' theme, similar to a Mister Softee ice-cream van, and the image would have been complete. I used to feel very important sitting high up in the passenger seat, looking at the paperwork and telling Bill where the next drop-off address was to be. Quite often we would be offered a cup of tea by the outworkers, and at first Bill was not quite sure whether to accept their kind invitation because he did have the boss's son with him after all, and he was meant to be delivering, not supping hot beverages, but he soon relaxed into having me aboard with him and just said to me, "Not a word to Dad, eh!" I did not care what he did; he was in effect my boss whenever we were out delivering. I was not going to grass him up, besides I quite enjoyed stopping for a drink and a chat with the "ladies what stuck".

This was also quite a lucrative source of spare players for me as more often than not there would be a few rejects or just loose figures rolling around the back of the van. I did not care what team they were; into my pocket they went. They might come in useful one day and besides it was a perk of the job, I suppose. Friday afternoons were great, as this was pay day, and I was handed my pay packet along with all the other employees. It made me feel like part of the team, rather than the boss's son. I do believe Dad made sure it was done like this so I had no sense of being treated differently, which was very thoughtful of him.

The early and continued success of Subbuteo meant that Dad had the means to give me the best possible education and I had the whole private-school treatment from the very start. Pre-prep, prep school and eventually the public-school system, which I was led to believe was a privileged form of education, but you could have fooled me as I hated very minute of it, especially the public-school part. My personal belief is that there is no grey area in one's appreciation of the public-school system, it's black or white, loathe it or love it. I was very much in the black camp but I am not suggesting for one moment that the schools I attended were anything but excellent; they were the best that money could buy. The trouble was, and this was very much the case with my prep school, expectations of me were very much heightened because of who my father was and what he had achieved in a relatively short period of time.

My prep school was Holmewood House, one of the top schools of its type in the country. It also happened to be in Langton Green and a good many of the masters from the school used to gather in the local pub, The Greyhound as it was called then, to unwind after a hard day's teaching the privileged. More often than not Dad frequented the same establishment and very soon they became part of a regular drinking circle, which looking at it from my point of view was a conflict of interests. Dad's favourite tipple on these occasions was what he liked to call "gin and mixed" but was officially called gin and Italian.

It was a rather sickly concoction of gin and sweet and dry vermouth, but what made this drink special for Dad was the obligatory maraschino cherry on a cocktail stick, preferably the kind that was made of clear plastic in the shape of a sword, but a wooden one would suffice at a pinch. But it was the cherry which was of the utmost importance. God help any barman who happened to omit the cherry from his drink.

One of the masters in the drinking circle at the local pub also happened to be the headmaster of Holmewood House and he was a rather intimidating character. Well, to me he was. He always seemed to make sarcastic comments to me and I could never understand why. He was certainly one of those people who in my opinion were, to use a well-known euphemism, of questionable parentage. I could never take to him and was always telling Dad about my dislike for him. He told me that I must not be disrespectful as he was my headmaster. Of course I shouldn't. However, my headmaster played a significant part when it came to deciding which public-school I would be moving to, even if it was a rather underhand and unconventional method.

Being born and brought up a Roman Catholic and all that involves, Dad wanted me to go to a Catholic public-school, and my name was put down at a very early age to go to Worth Priory, near Crawley in West Sussex. The school, being part of Worth Abbey, was run by Benedictine monks, and was the epitome of a very good Catholic school. Without going into the rather complicated exam procedure that getting into public-school involves, I narrowly missed the pass mark set by Worth. But the headmaster advised Dad over a few glasses of whisky at the pub that he was confident that the pass mark I achieved would certainly be good enough to gain entry to a certain number of other public-schools, but they would not be of the Catholic persuasion. Mr Headmaster then suggested to Dad that if he was prepared to make a substantial financial contribution to the new cricket pavilion at his school, he would make sure that my exam papers were sent to a suitable school and that my admission would be guaranteed. Dad agreed to this and within days handed over a cheque for £250 towards the pavilion. Bribery and corruption were alive and well, and palms well greased in the private education system and that was how I ended up attending Eastbourne College.

The year 1966 was, of course, significant for all English football fans, but it was also a year that saw contrasting emotions for Dad personally and Subbuteo as a company. As far as Subbuteo was concerned, the World Cup saw sales soar beyond anyone's expectations, thanks in no small way to Sammy, who saw the enormous commercial potential of England hosting the World Cup.

Dad, at first, was for some reason reluctant to believe it would be that beneficial to Subbuteo and was not prepared to invest one penny in extra advertising and promotion of the game leading up to and during the tournament itself. He was talked round by Sammy's salesman's patter and it was by mutual agreement that the first ever television advert for Subbuteo should appear during the World Cup tournament at enormous expense. Sammy was confident that it would be worth the investment and that the cost would be easily covered by the extra sales the advert would generate.

He also rallied his sales team around him for the big push on the many retailers now springing up and convinced them to place extra orders for the game and its accessories as they were sure to experience a massive increase in demand. In turn, many of these retailers, wanting to make sure that they would sell their extra stock, set up window displays dedicated entirely to Subbuteo and the World Cup. It seemed that the nation's high streets and shopping centres were bathed in the glow of Subbuteo green! Sales were on the rise just because of the World Cup, but England actually winning the thing sent interest in football in general and Subbuteo in particular through the roof. It was way beyond even Sammy's expectations and Dad had to concede that he was right from the very start and in his own backhanded way apologised for doubting Sammy's initial enthusiasm.

Not only was the game riding on a crest of a wave with many football fans, Dad was even contacted by two or three of the England players who wanted to know if the company wanted them to endorse the game. They realised very quickly that their winning the World Cup had boosted Subbuteo's profile and it was a bandwagon on which they wanted to jump to make money for themselves. Normally, if a company wants any sort of celebrity endorsement it takes a great deal of time and effort to secure this type of service, but Subbuteo had them knocking on the door almost desperate to get involved. For some unaccountable reason Dad wanted nothing at all to do with this and turned down their overtures for sponsorship. Maybe it was the cost involved or maybe it was that he felt that somehow it would diminish his control over the game. I think it was probably that he felt no endorsement was necessary as Subbuteo had more or less become a self-promoting product. It was certainly good enough to be that. When Dad mentioned to Mum and me that these players had been in touch and he did not wish to play ball with them, I remember being really cross and disappointed with him as I would have loved the opportunity to meet them in the flesh, but it was not to be.

As Subbuteo grew after the World Cup, so did the staffing levels – a necessary overhead which needed to be implemented if the whole operation was to run as smoothly as possible. Dad was not only running the business, making day-to-day decisions on practically everything that cropped up, he found that he was even typing his own correspondence, which was indeed a very time consuming exercise. He was a whizz on the old manual typewriter. He was, however, able to use only two fingers, but he could make the typewriter steam with the speed he typed. If only he could have utilised all available fingers he would not have been looking to employ a personal secretary.

An advert was placed in the local newspaper for a suitable candidate to help Dad with all his paper-work. The response for this post was phenomenal and he must have spent a good week interviewing all prospective candidates. Eventually, after a lot of deliberation and ironically some consultation with Mum, he engaged the services of a local woman. I emphasise the word 'woman' as she was no spring chicken. She was probably in her late forties and certainly not the archetypal dolly-bird secretary. I shall just refer to her as Mrs Z for reasons which will hopefully become clear and obvious.

Almost immediately she was appointed she gave off an air of being superior to all the other employees and strutted around the place issuing orders to all and sundry, although without any authority. Being Peter Adolph's secretary seemed to go to her head. For some strange reason Dad appeared to realise how she was behaving and chose to ignore her antics as if he condoned her false air of superiority. He was totally taken in by her, in more ways than one and gave her too much respect and authority. She was getting her feet firmly under the table and was becoming more and more of an influence in Subbuteo and in Dad's life. She travelled with him to meetings even if an overnight stay was required, and let it be known that of course there were to be separate bedrooms. I think at first this was the case, but as time went on the company expense account was saved a bit of money by them sharing a room.

Mum knew nothing about what was going on. Yes, Dad told her that Mrs Z went to meetings with him, but the overnight stays were on his own. No one at Subbuteo had a clue what was going on and if any employee so much as said a bad word against her Dad would defend her to the hilt, justified or not. Surely that might have been a little insight into what was now becoming a fully-fledged extramarital relationship. The situation was a cliché. Successful businessman knocking around with his secretary, to put it mildly.

At home all was not well as far as Dad was

concerned, although neither of us guessed what was really happening. I noticed, and I am sure that Mum must have too, that Dad was not himself, although we could not quite put our finger on what was wrong. He was spending longer away from home and when he did honour us with his presence he was moody and not at all communicative. Mum tried as hard as she could to talk to him, and expressed her concern for his change of personality, but he just did not want to discuss anything, saying that he was fine, business was doing well and that she had nothing to be worried about and that it must be her imagination. It definitely wasn't, that's for sure. He was burying his head in the sand over something, or putting up his brick wall as I liked to call it. But Mum could not get to the bottom of it and her concern for him was growing by the day.

One Sunday afternoon in the late autumn of 1966, I noticed Dad packing up the car with wellington boots and other equipment and assumed he was getting ready to go out on one of his ornithological walks in the nearby countryside. So I went outside and asked him where he was going and, if he was going on a walk, could I go with him. That was unusual for me. I did not normally volunteer to go on any kind of walk, – if Mum and Dad were going I had to go with them, like it or not – but something inside of me felt that I wanted to get out. Yes, he was going out but he said that he would be going on his own and would I mind if I stayed at home with Mum, which was strange because he always welcomed company on his outings, and I thought he would jump at the chance of me going with him. Not this time. I was more or less dismissed and told to go back inside. Mum had no idea that he had planned to go out and seemed surprised that he had not mentioned it to her. This was not how he normally behaved.

Six o'clock came and it had now got dark and there was no sign whatsoever of Dad. Then seven o'clock and still no return. By eight o'clock I was getting ready for bed and still no Dad. I was getting very concerned, as you might imagine, and of course so was Mum.

She told me not to worry and that he had probably stopped off on his way home for a drink or something like that. I was not convinced by this reassurance and was sure that deep down she was just as worried as I was, but I settled down to sleep as best I could. I lay awake for what seemed ages, unable to sleep and listening out to hear the front door open. But all I could hear was Mum moving about restlessly downstairs.

Suddenly, I heard a car coming up the driveway and recognising the note of the engine realised at once it must be Dad. I looked at the clock beside my bed which told me it was ten fifteen and that Dad had been away from home for more than eight hours without a word. I heard Mum open a bottle of something and assumed it was a bottle of her favourite wine, judging by the pop of the cork. She must also have heard the car draw up and decided a drink was needed as she had no idea what to expect when Dad came through the front door.

The front door opened and I leapt out of bed, but

decided not to venture downstairs as I was a little afraid of what I might encounter. Instead I stood on the upstairs landing trying as hard as I could to hear what Dad and Mum were saying. I just had one of those gut feelings that something was about to come to a head over Dad's rather strange behaviour, but they shut the sitting-room door behind them and all I can remember hearing is muffled conversation coming from the other side. I found this rather frustrating and I distinctly recall thinking that, although I was only ten years old, I was part of this family and that I should be in on what they had to say to each other.

All of a sudden, I heard raised voices getting louder and louder all the time, and then there was a loud crash as if an object had been thrown across the room. I heard Mum scream and she opened the door and ran as fast as she could up the stairs, catching me standing on the landing. Her mouth was bleeding very heavily and she just said that Dad and her had had a grown-ups' argument and that I was not to worry and try to go back to sleep. I ran downstairs, leaving Mum to clean her mouth in the bathroom, and went into the sitting room to find Dad sitting on a chair, head in his hands, sobbing his eyes out. Now, I have to be honest. I do not know for sure if Mum's injured mouth was a result of the flying object or that Dad had actually hit her in a fit of rage and I never want to know. I would hate to think that Dad was the type of man to hit a woman. It was not in his nature.

Her mouth cleaned up, Mum came downstairs where he was still sobbing and I was sent back up to bed. Despite all the disruption I eventually drifted off to sleep. The next day I sat down with Mum and Dad and they explained to me as best they could what the previous night had been all about. Dad had just returned from seeing the doctor. It turned out that he had suffered a nervous breakdown and the previous evening it had all come to the surface. He could not explain what had caused the breakdown, and it would have been easier to cope with if he could.

The doctor prescribed some medication, which Dad was reluctant to take because he loathed taking any form of medicine and would rather let things run their own course. But this time, for his own good, he had to obey the doctor. It is difficult to explain exactly how I felt over this episode, but suffice to say I can remember being extremely frightened, and the visions of that evening have remained with me ever since.

The medication Dad was taking seemed to take effect very quickly and he was soon back on the road to recovery. Apparently, these things just happen sometimes, but in my opinion there is no smoke without fire as the old adage goes, and as time went on we were able to reflect on this period in Dad's life and see that it all made complete sense.

Dad was spending more time outside work hours with Mrs Z, telling Mum he was working late, a very flimsy excuse as all she had to do was to either phone across to his office or if necessary make the short trip across the road to actually investigate for herself had she felt so inclined. But he managed to get away with it somehow.

Mrs Z was always courteous to me on the occasions

I met her, but even at my young age I realised there was something about her I did not like and I always felt uneasy in her presence. If ever I mentioned my mum to her she seemed to twist the conversation around to another subject as if she was frightened to get too involved in anything to do with Mum. To an adult this would eventually appear to be a little on the strange side, but a child would be none the wiser, I suppose.

The years went by with Dad carrying on this double life, Mum and I being none the wiser, although I do recall at times asking Mum things like why was Daddy not in for dinner and was Daddy at his office. But Mum never suspected anything as he was a busy man with his own thriving business, and working unsocial hours and not being around at the same time every day were par for the course for anyone in his position.

It was a chance meeting in 1968 with a friend of Mum's, who said she saw Dad's car parked outside a house on a housing estate in the village, that started the alarm bells ringing in Mum's head. At the time his car was spotted he was supposed to have been at a meeting with a colleague at a pub in Tunbridge Wells. He told Mum he would have his dinner out. When Mum questioned this he told her that he had to stop off at his secretary's house on the way to his supposed meeting to collect some paperwork she had been working on at home. Call it a woman's intuition, but for the first time Mum had cause to disbelieve his excuse. She pushed the point further with him, refusing to believe his story and again he told her that she had no grounds for concern. He was backed into a corner and suddenly screamed at her for not believing in him and another almighty argument ensued, again with me in the background witnessing all that was going on.

It was a *déjà vu* situation, only this time Dad eventually cracked after what seemed hours, but was probably only twenty minutes or so, of a screaming argument. He sat down and confessed all that had been going on and that was why he had to have medication from the doctor for a nervous breakdown. In retrospect it all seemed so very obvious, but hindsight is a very wonderful gift, and if everyone had it, it would certainly make our lives a lot easier.

It seems pointless to mention that Mum was totally devastated by Dad's revelations, that should be taken as read, but her first reaction was to insist that Dad dismiss Mrs Z as his secretary at Subbuteo. As if he was not in enough bother, he refused point-blank Mum's very reasonable request.

That created even more tension between them and it was very quickly decided, by both parties, that it would be best for all concerned if Dad moved out of the family home and found some temporary accommodation until the dust had settled on this quite miserable episode.

Then they could look at the situation with more clarity and decide on the future together. I think deep down that despite being hurt very badly Mum knew exactly which side her bread was buttered, and that my own situation had to be considered very carefully as well. She was sensible enough to realise that any decision taken in the heat of the moment could turn out to be the wrong one.

The most logical place for Dad to live, bearing in mind he still needed to be in close proximity to the Subbuteo offices and factories, and also to have as much access to me as possible, was at the offices themselves. The offices were still very much set up as a residence where Dad and his mother had lived previously. So he set up his temporary home on the top floor of Upper Birchetts. Although it was quite comfortable and he was in very familiar surroundings, it was not a patch on what he was used to, living at home with Mum and me. But he made the best of a bad situation.

To be fair, Mum never once refused Dad access to see me. I would often go over to his place at the offices for the evening and maybe he would take me out for an evening meal, and even if there was a while between us being in contact, he would always send a letter over to Little Pryors to let me know how he was getting on.

Despite being able to see Dad more or less whenever I wanted, it was not the most normal or indeed stable of situations to be caught in the middle of. I was thirteen years old at the time and that is a bad enough time for any young man, what with the start of the raging hormones and all that involves. I was also on the verge of leaving my prep school and going on to boarding school at Eastbourne College, which in itself is a time of massive change and upheaval. Well, it was for me.

As far as I am concerned, boarding school is a

barbaric institution and is more or less legalised child abuse and should be outlawed. I started boarding at the relatively late age of fourteen, but some children are separated from their parents and family unit and sent off to these institutions as young as eight years old. Some people swim and some people sink under these circumstances, depending a great deal on how they are raised within their families. I think, looking back, that my main reason for not settling at boarding school had a lot to do with the fact that I was an only child, and not used to being thrust into a situation where it is imperative you are comfortable and familiar with being around others and having to interact with them, share facilities with them and generally engage in all kinds of normal social activities. Not having any siblings, this was a way of life which was completely alien to me and the situation that was prevailing on the home front between Mum and Dad did not help matters either, I'm sure.

Starting at boarding school was a traumatic experience. I found it really difficult to settle in and make friends. Unlike my previous school, no one was aware, to my knowledge anyway, of the Subbuteo connection, so I am unable to put down any hostility towards me as being because of jealousy or anything like that. It sounds a strange thing to say but I believe that boys of that age will find any small thing to latch onto to make life a little difficult for other boys if they are that way inclined. It did not take long at all for things to start to get on top of me, and one afternoon, I decided on the spur of the moment that I had had enough and ran away. I put on my weekend casual clothes and when everyone was off playing rugby I started walking into the town centre and made my way as quickly as I could to the main road that led out of the town.

I had no idea at all what I was planning to do, as I was thirty-five miles from home. All I wanted to do was get away from school. An hour or so later it was starting to get dark and I was a couple of miles away from school when I devised a plan which I thought would get me home by the early evening. I had the foresight to put a small amount of loose change in my pocket which was left over from the previous week's pocket money allowance. Having stopped walking for a short while I had a quick count up and realised that I had just enough money, probably, to catch a bus back to Tunbridge Wells, but not from where I was just outside Eastbourne.

I saw a row of houses ahead of me and walked up to the first one and knocked on the door. An elderly gentleman answered and I think he was surprised to see a young man on his own standing in front of him. I asked him if he could help me and made up a story that I had been on a day trip with my parents to Eastbourne, managed to get lost and separated from them and could he please drive me to the next town so I could catch a bus home. This was a totally unbelievable story but I was by now desperate to get home and I just said anything. The gentleman invited me into his home where his wife was waiting and wondering what on earth was going on. He expressed his doubts as to the validity of my half-baked story.

I told him that it was all true but I very soon realised that to keep up the pretence was futile and I told the truth. He was very understanding and offered to phone my housemaster, Mr Young, to see if he could come and collect me. With a great deal of trepidation and concern as to how my antics were to be received by my housemaster, I waited patiently to be collected from my house of refuge. Surprisingly, my concerns were unfounded and I was shown a great deal of compassion and understanding concerning my unhappiness at school. I was told that I was not the first and would probably not be the last to act as I did. Mum and Dad were contacted by phone and I spoke with Dad for what seemed ages about my problem settling in to my new and alien surroundings.

The upshot was that Mum wanted to take me away from Eastbourne College at once and try to get me a placement in a local school for my own well-being, but Dad took the completely opposite stance and maintained that although he could entirely understand my feelings and predicament, I must try to stick it out, learn how to cope and make an effort to integrate, muck in and make friends. Apparently, by doing this, I would be a stronger and better person.

Dad got his wish and I was stuck at boarding school for the next four years, although I do admit as time went on I slowly but surely got used to my surroundings. I have to begrudgingly admit that by my fourth and last year, life at boarding school was at least quite tolerable. Being a senior meant that there were a certain amount of unwritten privileges of which you could take advantage, such as getting the first years to run around after you, making cups of coffee or piles of buttered toast after games, that kind of thing. To all intents and purposes it was the old public-school fagging system and although that had been officially outlawed just before I arrived it was still the same ploy that was implemented by the senior pupils. Except now it was called 'doing duties'. What's in a name?

One of the first years who used to knock on my study door to ask if I needed anything was a young man who went by the name of Edward Izzard. You may know him nowadays as Eddie Izzard, the renowned comedian, who I believe was once quoted as saying that he was "a lesbian trapped in a man's body".

Anyway, after four years it was my time to leave and I couldn't get out of there quick enough. But I have to say that despite my utter dislike of the whole experience, in retrospect I am pleased that Dad stuck to his guns and didn't pull me out, because in a strange way I do actually feel proud and indeed honoured to have been part of the English public-school system and all that it stands for – even today.

Chapter 4

Playing Subbuteo – My Story

MY OWN EXPERIENCE and stories of playing Subbuteo are probably no different from the millions of people worldwide who have ever played the game. The only difference is that many of my games were played against the inventor.

From a very early age I was surrounded by all things Subbuteo, and even before I could fully understand what these strange little figures were for, I was handling them, putting them in my mouth, as babies and toddlers do, and generally playing with them in every possible way, but not as Dad had intended.

It is a miracle that I never had to be rushed to hospital to have a little plastic man on a base removed from my throat or one surgically removed with a pair of tweezers from my nose. I started playing in a way which vaguely resembled the correct way when I was about three or four and that was with coaching from the man himself. Start them young seemed to be the order of the day.

Of course, being very young, the word Subbuteo was rather a strange and difficult word to get my tongue around, so I innocently came up with a phrase that described the game that I was so cack-handedly trying to play. That phrase – 'Knock Another One Over' – has stuck with me. It became a kind of family catchphrase. "Daddy, can we play knock another one over?" was a cry that went up many a time in the Adolph household. I think only a young child could have come up with such a logical description of the game. Logical in my eyes at least, as that was exactly what I was doing.

At such a tender age, no attempt to hit the little ball was made at all. I just wanted to knock over all the men. I suppose to some degree it resembled American Football – now there's an idea! – rather than the beautiful game we all know and love. It might have taken many man-hours and a great deal of money for a company advertising department to come up with a suitable slogan to describe the game of Subbuteo, if indeed a slogan was needed at all, which it was not.

Up until the age of about ten, my grasp of the finer points of the game increased steadily and my skill levels, although I say it myself, were going through the roof for one so relatively young. I know that children of that age were playing the game, but in my experience there was none of the subtlety involved, subtlety I seemed to have grasped. Many of my contemporaries at school had no idea of the flicking technique which was involved, which as any self-respecting Subbuteo player will know, is to use the middle or index finger and employ the pitch and not the thumb as leverage.

The technique, if it can be called that, which used to get me so irate (it still does to this very day if I see it being used) is the one whereby the index finger is bent in an L shape and used to scrape, for want of a better word, the player towards the ball. For one, it does not allow the figure to spin if required and from an aesthetic point of view it looks downright ugly. I realise I am being totally petty here, but I am sure any half-decent Subbuteo player would agree with me on these points. I was bought up as a Subbuteo purist and I will remain one until the day I die.

Mentioning techniques employed by my school chums brings me neatly to the time when I was first introduced to competitive Subbuteo. I call it competitive yet, as you will shortly find out, it was anything but. I suppose I was about twelve years old, so the year must have been 1968 and I was attending the fee-paying prep school in the village of Langton Green. It was during the summer term and the end of a PE lesson:

"Adolph, meet me in the common room at break-time, please."

The voice of the PE teacher boomed across the gym as we were packing up various items of apparatus.

"Er, yes, OK, Sir" I replied, not quite knowing what I had done wrong, if anything. I could not concentrate at all during my next lesson, trying to work out why I had been summoned to see my PE teacher.

Breaktime came and I made my way to the masters' common room, knocked on the door and rather anxiously awaited the order to enter.

"Come in," came the reply after a bit of a wait.

I entered the inner sanctum where a gaggle of teachers were milling around drinking mugs of coffee.

"I've come to see Mr Woolmer," I said to the nearest teacher.

"Bob, someone to see you. Adolph, I think," he shouted across the room to the tracksuited one.

"Ah, Mark, come on in and take a seat," he said, pulling up a chair. Christian name terms, so it cannot be that serious.

He stared at me for a few seconds and then in a very friendly manner said, "Your father, he's the Subbuteo man, isn't he?"

"Yes, Sir, that's right," I replied.

"Well, I was wondering what you thought of starting a school Subbuteo league. Perhaps your father might be good enough to contribute a pitch and accessories and a few teams. What do you think?"

I thought this sounded a fantastic idea, especially as I knew I had a fair chance of winning something at school at long last. A little unfair maybe, but winning is winning after all. I told Mr Woolmer that I would have a chat with my father when I got home that evening and see what we could come up with.

I would like to mention at this point, by way of a small digression, that this Mr Woolmer, or Bob Woolmer as he was better known outside school, went on to play county cricket for Kent and, I believe, England, and at the time of writing is coach to the Pakistan team.

I say believe because I'm afraid cricket is not one of my strongest subjects, in fact without wishing to offend any cricket puritans out there, the only positive thing about cricket, in my ever so humble opinion, is that it is an exceedingly effective cure for insomnia. Now, you get me on the subject of football and it's a completely different story.

That evening I summoned Dad to a meeting (which sounds a very grand thing for a twelve-year-old boy to do, but he was a very busy man and needed to be pinned down) to discuss the proposition put to me earlier in the day by my PE teacher. After some buttering up, Dad agreed to supply any items required for our school league. By buttering up, I mean I allowed him to beat me by at least five clear goals in a game of Subbuteo. I have to say that at this stage in my Subbuteo playing, I was still unable to beat him but my losses to him were only by the odd goal or two, never cricket scores. However I figured that a large score in his favour might massage his ego a little. Also a casual remark complimenting him on his inswinging corners wouldn't do any harm either. He had this amazing technique for scoring direct from a corner kick, something I have yet to master even to this present day. It's all to do with the wrist action or so I am told.

Anyway, having been humiliated by a false and contrived 6-1 defeat, a consolation goal being scored by me in the final minute, Dad agreed to let me loose in the factory storeroom to lay my hands on any equipment I deemed necessary for our new school Subbuteo league. I managed to obtain a playing cloth, two goals, half a dozen teams and a handful of assorted sized balls in three different colours, orange, brown and white. I have always favoured using the medium-sized balls myself, but a selection was chosen to cater for all eventualities and preferences.

The next day I transported my loot to school and presented them to a very pleased and delighted Mr Woolmer, who then set about the task of getting as many interested boys as he could to take part in the inaugural school Subbuteo league. Eventually, about twelve boys, including me of course, signed up for the league, which was to take place every Friday afternoon after school and to be held using only one table, in the school gym. It was agreed, as an extra favour by Dad, that the first match of the league would be kicked off by him, to add a bit of a ceremonial touch to the proceedings. A kind of opening ceremony, I suppose you could call it.

The league got under way and I think everyone involved looked forward to Friday afternoons to play their matches. I did not, as a rule, involve myself too much in after-school activities, despite a lot of cajoling and encouragement from my parents telling me that I must try to "muck in more". This was a favourite expression of Dad's and one which got on my nerves. The school Subbuteo league was, of course, a situation I was only too keen to muck in with and halfway through the season I found myself top of the league, having lost not one match.

To be totally honest, I found the whole thing a bit of a pushover. The second half of the season continued and opponents came and went, beaten quite easily, and by the timeit finished at the end of term I was crowned runaway champion, having dropped only three points. That was three draws and no losses, and this was when two points were awarded for a win and not three as it is nowadays. It was certainly a good feeling to have won something at school at long last, but I have to admit to feeling slightly unchallenged by the whole event. Despite this, I was keen to know if the league would be continuing again the following term and so I approached Mr Woolmer to ask. To my considerable dismay I was informed that due to my overwhelming success in the inaugural season, and to give the others a chance of winning, I was banned from the following term's league. What a cheek! I could not believe what I was hearing. That's currently the equivalent of Jose Mourinho being told that Chelsea were banned from competing in the Premiership due to the fact that they were too good, and didn't give any other club the chance to win something.

Having mulled over the situation, it occurred to me that this was in a strange way a backhanded compliment. I vowed to accept the decision gracefully and, so as not to appear mean, allowed my pitch and accessories to be used by the school for future leagues. That was big of me, but at the age of twelve, it seemed a very mature attitude indeed.

It was not long after this episode that the bitter pill of banishment was sweetened somewhat by an announcement from Dad that he was toying with the idea of starting a league of his own, drawing on some players among his staff. He asked me what I thought of the idea and would I like to play in it, and perhaps invite a few of my friends to participate. What do you think my answer was? Here was a chance to test my Subbuteo skills against the 'big boys'. I was already playing Dad quite regularly, but never played anyone else whose skill level was of a high standard. When I played Dad, there were plenty of tears and tantrums from me on occasions, not because I was a bad loser or even at the frustration of never quite being able to beat him, but always in the manner that I lost. Dad sometimes cheated. I have to say it was more to wind me up in an affectionate, playful manner than to win by unfair advantage, as he had no reason to cheat whatsoever. He played with me like a cat plays with a mouse.

I have to say that at times his shots were so hard and fast that the ball entered the goal at such speed that they came back out again so that I never even saw them. "Missed!" I used to shout. "Never, that was a good goal if ever there was one," came his reply. Of course, the opposite used to occur, when one of these shots narrowly missed the goal and rebounded back onto the pitch from the fence surround and Dad claimed a goal. I should mention at this point, that I had a custom-made chipboard pitch with an inch-high wooden surround, expertly dovetailed at the corners with the baize playing surface glued onto the board.

To add a little realism, I used to cut out adverts from various magazines, trim them to size and cover the whole surround. If I'd played on the floor like any normal kid of that age, none of this rebound business would have occurred. I soon got so fed up with these false claims for a goal, or not a goal, that I started to implement the 'sticky tape in back of net' system to stamp out cheating and controversy once and for all. And it seemed to have a positive effect on our future games together, much to Dad's annoyance. After all, it was his idea in the first place to get a two-inch wide piece of common or garden sticky tape, package it in the Subbuteo green livery, give it a catalogue reference number and flog it to the kids as a new and innovative device for keeping the ball in the back of the net. And it sold like hot cakes. I have to confess that I have always been of the opinion that anyone actually spending their hard-earned cash on this rather dubious accessory was stretching product loyalty to the limit!

To gauge the level of interest in the proposed league, word was put about by Dad among his staff and a notice was pinned up for interested parties to add their names. The response was positive with around twenty staff members registering to compete. But Dad had decided that the league should consist of only eight players. Any more would certainly have been too many as it was agreed that the league should take place once a week for a couple of hours, with each match having fifteen minutes each half. The criteria for choosing eight from twenty was based on expertise, as I think Dad wanted the league to be of a fairly high standard.

Eventually, the final eight were decided upon and if you could allow me a bit of indulgence at this juncture, I would like to test the old grey matter and list the names of the players and their chosen team. They were, in no particular order: My dad (QPR), George Underwood (Arsenal), Richard Watt, a good friend of mine (Chelsea), Charlie Rice, a friend from school (Manchester United), Graham Bridges, the son of Ken Bridges, home workers' manager, or 'outworkers' as we liked to call them (Celtic), Sam Till, assembly operative (West Ham), John Hyder, delivery driver (Spurs) and me, Mark Adolph (Manchester City). I was then and still am to this day a devout QPR fan like Dad, but at this particular stage in my life I took a great deal of pleasure from taking up a contrary position to Dad with regard to which football team I followed. I chose Manchester City for no good reason except they were a top club and this was the era of Colin Bell, Francis Lee, Mike Summerbee and Joe Corrigan etc.

Our league was soon up and running and we normally met on Tuesday evenings in Dad's office in the main Subbuteo complex. Actually, to describe it as a complex is a bit grand really, for in reality it was a large extension of Dad's mother's house where Dad used to live before he was married. Most of the rooms were used as offices for accountants, bookkeepers and order processing. Dad's office was part of the extension, with a large factory area above which everyone called "the store".

It was where all the games and teams were assembled, ready for onward transit to numerous retail outlets across the country. It was a very large office with pine-clad walls and wood-block flooring with four very large windows overlooking the rear garden of the house. It was more like an executive conservatory to be honest. Still, it was an ideal size for holding our league in and without the necessity of moving any office furniture around.

It was agreed that to make our league more

competitive and realistic, everyone would play each other on a home and away basis during the season, but the only problem was, and I am sure it is one which is shared by many leagues still operating to this day, that all games are played at the same venue and using the same pitch so the literal home and away fixture did not apply. How were we to get over this and give the 'home' team an advantage as in real football? Well, someone came up with the bright idea of having a home-team penalty.

Guess who that someone was? Dad, of course. To be fair it was a good idea, but even if it hadn't been there was certainly no one who was going to stand up and tell him so. Certainly not any of the staff players anyway. I might have been able to tell him because I was not beholden to him for a living. How this idea worked was that the designated home team would take a penalty prior to the kick-off of the match, from anywhere inside the semicircle on the edge of the penalty area. If this penalty was scored, the home player would start the match a goal to the good. I believe there is a saying in football circles that home advantage and good support are worth a goal start. I believe our small deviation from normal Subbuteo rules in some way brought that saying to life and it undoubtedly added a certain edge and realism to our matches.

I personally found this league a great deal more challenging than the one from which I had been banned at school and I lost my two matches against Dad, one by a single goal in his home match which ironically would have been a 0-0 draw had he not introduced that stupid and really useless concept of the home advantage penalty, and the other 2-1 at home. The season ended and everyone seemed to have enjoyed themselves immensely, but there are no prizes for guessing who finished top. I was a respectable third, which sounds all right I suppose, but out of eight players, just above halfway – well, I was pleased. The player who finished bottom, who shall remain nameless, kept us all amused and a little frustrated week in and week out by never quite grasping the idea that when keeping goal one had to place a finger on the crossbar to stop the goal moving when saving a shot. These were the early free-standing goals we were using and they had no facility for securing them to the pitch by way of a couple of drawing pins. Most weeks his inability to hold his goal steady resulted in it flying across Dad's office and no one knowing what the outcome was. No wonder this player took the relegation position. Relegation to where I don't know, but he certainly became the butt of everyone's jokes. Oh, go on then, it was... No, I said I wouldn't reveal his name, but if he ever reads this I am sure he will recognise himself.

One of the most common questions I get asked is, can I remember the first time that I beat Dad in a game of Subbuteo? For some strange reason this always seems to remind me of the one when you are asked if you can remember what you were doing when Kennedy was assassinated, when Elvis died or when John Lennon was shot. Please don't misunderstand me, I am not comparing those events to my first triumph over Dad in any way at all, God forbid. It is just one of those questions that has always been repeated throughout my life. The answer is, yes, of course I can remember, and a treasured memory it is too. I suppose, to my way of thinking, it was my Subbuteo coming of age and from that moment on I always felt psychologically that I had moved up to the next level of play.

The moment in question happened not long after the aforementioned league had finished, which if it had happened a little earlier it might have put me higher in the league. It was on a Sunday evening not long before Christmas 1968, and I had that Sunday night feeling, knowing that I had another week at school before the Christmas holidays started. Dad could see that I was a little down in the dumps and he asked me if I fancied a game of Subbuteo, or to be more precise he asked me in his usual fashion "Do you want a thrashing?" which to an outsider who had just joined the conversation might have appeared to have had more sinister connotations. But of course I fully understood this very familiar request and as usual took it in its literal sense, not anticipating in any way a deviation from the normal course of events. Tomorrow morning the sun will rise; tonight Dad will beat me at Subbuteo. Both these events were foregone conclusions it would seem, but as it transpired the sun, on this particular occasion, struggled to appear over the horizon.

Dad automatically chose to be QPR and I was Manchester City, as normal. The first half ended with Dad leading 1-0. We always played ten minutes each half, or each way as Dad preferred to call it.

This being timed on a kitchen egg timer, not the sand-filled device obviously, but one which made an awful racket when it went off, a little like a fire alarm. (I think that Subbuteo sold a gadget similar to this as an accessory – an everyday object sold in Subbuteo packaging, a little like the previously mentioned sticky tape.)

The second half got under way and within minutes I scored an equaliser, a rather scrappy goal as I recall but they all count, as the old football adage goes. Time was ticking away and a draw seemed very much on the cards, when suddenly Dad made a horrendously mistimed and uncharacteristic defensive error and left me a clear, long-range shot which I took, if you don't mind me blowing my own trumpet, magnificently! These are the type of shots that have the capability of looking spectacular if pulled off, or alternatively making you look a complete idiot if you don't connect with them properly. Luckily for me, the former happened and the ball was struck just off centre.

It flew, very low, into the corner of Dad's goal. The sticky tape did its job, as did the drawing pins holding down the new-style goal I had started using. And there I was a goal to the good with only a minute or so left on the clock. A momentous occasion was about to happen, and when the timer went off to signal the end of the game I heaved a sigh of relief that at long last my duck against Dad had been broken.

Dad was very gracious after his first defeat by me, and I am sure that he knew how much it meant to me. But rest assured that not all future defeats he suffered at my hands were accepted with such grace. The gloves were off now and he realised that beating me was now no longer a foregone conclusion, that he had to raise his game if he was to continue having the upper hand in our matches.

This had a knock-on effect because as he raised his game I followed suit and tried my hardest to match him. I now found that having beaten Dad for the first time my enthusiasm for playing Subbuteo was taken to a higher level. It was a major breakthrough as far I was concerned and I decided that I needed to practise my skills as often as possible to keep them honed. I knew that Subbuteo produced a range of practice accessories, and I needed to lay my hands on all of them as soon as possible. There were the dribbling posts, a shooting practice accessory, which was a yellow-coloured contraption that fitted over the goal mouth with five holes in it slightly larger than a ball.

It was not dissimilar to the kind of football shooting game one can often come across at a fairground or a village fete. Three scores and win a cuddly toy or a goldfish in a plastic bag, that sort of thing. There was a device designed to help improve passing skills which was basically a smaller version of the office putting-game for bored executives, a green plastic disc, approximately three inches in diameter, with a hole in the centre to trap the ball, and finally there was the goalkeeping rebound board, a piece of goal-sized plastic with elastic bands stretched tightly across it to simulate the ball being shot while you kept goal. This looked a very basic piece of equipment, but it really did work well, with the ball coming back at you very fast indeed and from every conceivable angle.

Being allowed to go to the store and to choose a new team or accessory was always a thrill for me. I suppose an outsider would think it was just a case of going in whenever the fancy took me and helping myself to whatever I wanted. Dad was the boss after all. That was far from the truth. I always had to approach Dad when I felt he was in a good mood and put my case forward as to why I thought I deserved a trip to the store. I had to say exactly what I wanted, and it was never a case of going in and having a free rein. I suppose looking at it now from his viewpoint, although I was his son, he still had a business to run and it would not have looked very good among his staff to have me running around the store helping myself to everything in sight.

The store was situated directly above Dad's office and it was used not only for the storage of assembled games and teams but also for the physical assembly of these items. Outside access to these premises was via a large wrought-iron staircase, with a small landing halfway up and another at the top, a little like a fire-escape, but it was not designed for that purpose. It was on this top landing some thirty-five years later that I stood chatting with television presenter Chris Tarrant, while I was filming with him for a documentary series he was making for ITV. To this very day, in my mind I can still hear the very distinctive sound of people clattering up and down this staircase and it always brings back very strong and happy memories of that particular era in

Subbuteo, a little like a specific smell can conjure up certain memories.

On one occasion I recall asking Dad if I could have a new team, and for some reason I seem to remember it being the Manchester City away strip, which at that particular time was red and black stripes with black shorts. Instead of the usual "Yes, but how can you justify this request?" routine, Dad told me that due to a staff shortage they were very behind in getting a despatch ready and would I like to help out for an afternoon on the assembly line in return for my much sought after Manchester City away team.

I readily agreed to this as I thought it would be quite interesting and in some way a bit of fun, and would also help pass a bit of time during the school holidays. So, the following afternoon, I met up with Dad in his office and we made our way up the wrought-iron staircase to the store, where we were greeted by a long-serving member of staff who went by the name of 'Nobby' Clarke. I could never understand why everyone called him Nobby, but was led to believe that anyone with the surname Clarke, with or without an 'e', was traditionally referred to by this nickname. I never did find out his real Christian name.

Nobby, or Mr Clarke, as I had respectfully to call him, was a very pallid-looking man in his late fifties, early sixties who had been working for Dad and Subbuteo since the year dot and seemed to stand out from other employees, to my mind anyway, because he always wore what I like to call arm garters, which were really expandable bracelets worn halfway up the forearm to keep the shirtsleeves above the wrist. On his head he always wore, come rain or shine, a peaked sun visor which made him look like he should be working in a casino in Las Vegas, not a Subbuteo factory in Langton Green.

Nobby was to take me under his wing for the afternoon and I was given the task of assembling referee and linesman accessory sets. I sat up at a workbench with two huge bags beside me, one containing approximately two thousand referee figures and in the other the same quantity in linesman figures and all that was required of me was to put one referee and two linesmen (I repeat, ONE referee and TWO linesmen) into a small polythene bag and then staple a green Subbuteo header card to seal it closed. I spent all afternoon mindlessly doing my job and chatting with Nobby, and I probably had assembled something in the region of one thousand sets of these accessories, when Dad rolled in and said that it was time to leave for the day. He started chatting with Nobby and asking how I had got on during the afternoon, casually picking up one of my assembled sets and pointing out to me that it had two referees and one linesman in it. "Never mind, just a one-off mistake. We all make them," he said. On closer inspection, Dad, his hands delving into the box like a lucky dip, realised that I had made the same error on every single one of the thousand or so sets. TWO referees and ONE linesman.

You can imagine how I felt. Dad was very understanding, in front of Nobby and the staff at least, and they all thought it highly amusing, but when Dad and I were on our own in his office a few moments later he did point out, in the nicest possible way, that if I wanted to do any more work to earn some pocket money or a new team, I would have to concentrate a little more.

He also made the fair point that if he had not checked my work, those accessories would have ended up in the shops and bought by the public, and that would not have done the image of Subbuteo any good at all. After all that, I did still manage to get my Manchester City away team, but only after returning the following afternoon to redress my horrendous error.

The practice accessories I was trying to get hold of were eventually acquired, but not quite in the manner I had planned. Following the referee and linesman débâcle, I decided that any future requests for freebies would have to be put on hold for a while, at least until the episode faded from Dad's memory slightly. I felt guilty about asking for anything.

I mentioned, very briefly earlier in this chapter, Richard Watt, a Chelsea supporter, but despite that a very good friend and marvellous Subbuteo player. I have known Richard since we were babies as our mothers were the best of friends in Langton Green. Our pre-teens friendship was spent not really playing Subbuteo too much, but indulging in a fantasy world of Action Man, collecting all the accessories and building up enough stars from the packs to send off for a free Action Man figure, which arrived by post completely naked except for a dog tag. At one point I think I must have had more Action

Man paraphernalia than I did Subbuteo teams, but that was soon to change.

Our friendship really blossomed when we were around thirteen or fourteen and we spent literally all of our school holidays playing Subbuteo. As I was at boarding school, the holidays were really the only time we could dedicate ourselves to our religion, which was Subbuteo. We played most of the time at Little Pryors in the 'big room' although I did venture to his house on occasions just to change the routine. At first, we started playing just friendly games but this started to get a little tedious so we started a two-division league system consisting of about twenty teams in total, and we managed (played with) ten or so teams each across both divisions. We didn't have the teams one would normally expect to have in our league.

We had some very unfashionable teams such as Hamilton Academicals, Dumbarton, Airdrie, Bradford City, Bournemouth. You get my drift. This was not done deliberately; it was just the teams I happened to have in my ever-growing collection. These teams were all kept readily to hand in sectioned off 00 scale team boxes and kept on top of the safe which was bolted to the concrete floor in the 'big room'. The league was a very even affair, neither of us particularly dominating, which of course made it interesting.

All matches were logged with scores and scorers, courtesy of every team having those fiddly small numbers on their backs, and even half-time scores with league tables being drawn up at the end of each round of matches. Richard always, without fail, had the laborious job of writing up the stats, as to be honest, his handwriting was more legible than mine. Well, that's my story and I'm sticking to it.

Cup competitions were drawn up using the bracket system, rather than doing a draw for each round. It was all very serious, and a great deal of my evenings were spent practising, especially if I knew I had a vital league or cup match coming up the next day. Sometimes, if he was not too busy, I would enlist Dad to help me practise, for example being in goal so that I could brush up on my shooting and vice versa to sharpen up my goalkeeping. This was under the strict understanding that Richard was not to get wind of our little training sessions. He might get the idea that I was gaining an unfair advantage. Of course I was, but all is fair in love and Subbuteo.

For cup finals, I even used a clothes brush to make a striped effect on the baize cloth, just like at Wembley. I tried doing circles but that was not as effective. Diagonal stripes looked good as well. If you haven't done so already, try it. It is most effective.

Most of the time, although very competitive, our games were conducted with a good deal of sportsmanship, but I lost one cup final and I recall going absolutely off the rails, sulking and not talking to Richard after the game.

So much so that Dad had to intervene and send Richard home for his own good, making me phone him later in the day to apologise. It was the only time that I really lost it and over what? A game of Subbuteo. That's all it was. But it felt a lot more important than that at the time, I can assure you. Surely I cannot have been the only person ever to have taken a game of Subbuteo so seriously.

At the risk of repeating myself, which I know I am, these aforementioned emotions and experiences are probably echoed by the millions of people who have ever played Subbuteo. If you have never had these experiences you have probably not been playing the game in the way in which it was intended.

Chapter 5

Cars and Other Passions

WARNING! The following piece of narrative may cause symptoms of boredom and severe bouts of yawning to the reader. Please feel totally free to skip this part of my story if you so wish. I admit that a long piece about the humble motor car in all its various shapes and sizes can be a little tedious to those of you with no interest at all in what is essentially a lump of metal whose main purpose is to transport us as safely and as quickly as possible from point A to point B.

For those of you who wish to stick with it because you have an interest in cars or you just want to get your money's worth from the purchase you have currently in your hand, I hope I am able to give you some insight into Dad's passion for cars. I remember my mum saying on numerous occasions that trying to get Dad to buy something as basic as, say, a washing machine was akin to extracting blood from the proverbial stone, but going out to buy a car or three was so easy and pleasurable. I do believe I may have inherited this particular gene because I am somehow able to buy a car with considerable ease, but if I need to buy a pair of socks, for example, I have to go away, sit down and have a cup of coffee and think about it. Sad but true.

During the late sixties, when Subbuteo was well and truly at its height, Dad decided to stray away from his normally, in my opinion anyway, excellent choice of cars. For some bizarre reason, known only to himself, he decided to buy three of the most ostentatious American cars imaginable, namely a Ford Thunderbird, a Chevrolet Chevelle convertible and a mammoth eight-litre Pontiac Firebird. All three were purchased new from an importer in London, all within about a month of each other and all were right-hand drive. The Thunderbird was truly tacky, with a black landau roof which looked as if it should retract à la convertible style but was, in fact, made of tough plastic and did nothing of the sort. It had what my mum used to describe as "knock-off wheels that didn't knock off".

I believe this was a reference to the old sports cars of the time, which had a large wing-nut contraption in the centre of the wheel, which, when hit with a hammer, facilitated the removal of the wheel very quickly. Anyway, the wheels on the Thunderbird had these winged nuts purely for effect, and the removal of the wheel was by undoing four nuts in the traditional way. In its favour, the leather interior was real and the rear doors hinged from the rear, not from the front in the usual manner, which made gaining access to the back seats rather confusing. The brake lights were typically American. Dad used to say that they played bingo when operated, meaning that they used to flash in sequence, left to right, until the pedal was released. Many a time he was pulled over by the boys in blue for not having lights that conformed and eventually had to have them replaced with a normal braking lights system. Of course, being the sixties, the car was equipped with an eight-track stereo system, all the rage at the time but a short-lived piece of technology which never really took off and was soon replaced by the audio cassette.

Many a long journey in this car was spent by me listening to the *Oliver* soundtrack on one continuous loop. As a side note, I still love the music from that show and film. Perhaps the journeys in the T-Bird were the start of it.

The Chevrolet Chevelle was, I have to admit, the nicest of the three. It was a white four-seater convertible with a matching white roof and black leather seats. It had good pose value which even I appreciated at the age of twelve, although I have to say that I remember feeling distinctly embarrassed at times when Dad used to come to school to pick me up in it, with the roof down. All my friends used to stop what they were doing and just stare at me getting into it. "Wow, look at Adolph's dad's car," they used say. I did not like all the attention.

This car actually made it onto Spanish television. Dad was driving through Spain on one of his many ornithological jaunts, and found himself by pure chance being one of the first cars to cross a newly-opened bridge. Realising that there were TV cameras recording the whole event he decided midway across to open electronically the roof of the Chevy. Back at his hotel that evening he watched his antics on a Spanish news programme. Although

Peter, second from left, lines up for Brentford schoolboys.

Peter with one of his treasured Bristol cars in the late 1950s.

Peter in cricket whites, circa 1930.

Singing with the Oscar Rabin Band in 1939.

Peter and Pam get married with his mother looking not very happy.

Where Subbuteo first began – the lodge in Langton Green.

The proud father in 1956.

The author as a trainee matador, with Jaguar.

On the QE2 in 1969.

A Subbuteo set in the grounds of Upper Birchetts, the first factory.

The Ford Thunderbird and Little Pryors.

*The ornithological expedition to Switzerland with E-Type Jaguar
in the early 1970s.*

basically a shy man, sometimes the showman in him came to the fore.

The Firebird was probably the ultimate muscle car – 8.2 litres to be precise with automatic transmission. It was midnight blue with beige leather seats. When driving this beast Dad was constantly being hassled by other drivers for a burn-up. Of course, they knew that really they could not compete, but it was the challenge of having a go. Except one time some 'boy racer' in a souped-up Ford Anglia – you know the sort, one with tractor wheels on the rear and pram wheels on the front and a shirt button masquerading as a steering wheel – decided to take on the Firebird for real while waiting at a set of traffic lights. There was lots of revving and noise coming from the Anglia, waiting for the lights to turn green. Green they went and off went the Anglia, wheels spinning and churning up the tarmac while Dad floored the right pedal of the Firebird. This was not a competition. After about one hundred yards with the Firebird hardly breaking sweat, the Anglia came to a grinding halt with steam billowing from its bonnet, and promptly blew up, quite literally. It took on the best and failed miserably. I am sure this young driver was firmly put in his place. Dad just smiled and carried on his way.

In August 1970, Mum took delivery of a brand-new Mercedes Benz 280 SE saloon in white. This was her pride and joy as she had always hankered after a Mercedes. She gave it the name of Ellie, as the registration letters were ELE. This was a practice Mum and Dad tried to do on all their cars. It was during my first few weeks at my new boarding school that I received a rather distraught letter from Mum, saying Dad had crashed the Merc. Of course, my main concern was for my Dad's well-being, and not knowing the full story, decided to get to the nearest payphone and call home to find out the details. It transpired that one evening after dinner, Dad had offered to put Ellie away into the garage to save Mum the bother.

But he was wearing a pair of mule-type slippers and he had to make his way across a wet piece of grass to the drive to get into the car. Starting the engine, his wet, slippered foot slipped off the brake pedal of the automatic Mercedes and straight onto the accelerator which shot the car at full throttle into the garage and it embedded itself into the rear wall, with a pile of bricks and masonry on the two-week old-Mercedes' bonnet.

When my mum heard the crash from inside the house, her immediate thoughts were how Dad was. When she found out that he was not hurt, just a little shocked and ashamed of himself, she burst into tears at the sight of her precious car buried in the garage wall. It is a testimony to strength and build quality of the Mercedes that, despite the velocity with which it had hit the garage wall, and initial appearances, the damage done to the front of the car was not that severe. The impact would have written off a car of lesser quality. It was duly repaired under the insurance, but it took Dad years and years of leg pulling to live down this incident.

The Jaguar E-Type was probably the most iconic car of the sixties, and anyone who was anyone was seen to be driving one. Film stars, pop and rock stars, even footballers all seemed to own one or at least aspire to. George Harrison owned a black V12 and I am sure that George Best must have had one and if not he should have.

Dad too got his in the early seventies, just after he sold Subbuteo to Waddington. It was a red V12 coupé and was quite magnificent. He bought it brand spanking new from a local Jaguar dealership in Tunbridge Wells. It had the lovely chrome wire wheels and wooden steering wheel. The works. If he could have put a personal plate on it in those days, I'm sure he would have done just to complete the whole picture.

It was impossible for him to drive around the area incognito as everyone recognised the car and knew it was him. Parking it anywhere, be it at the local shops or even just the local, caused an immense amount of interest and people could be found standing around it in admiration whenever he emerged from wherever he had been, asking him about it and on occasions asking him to lift the bonnet so that they could look inside the engine.

Being around fourteen or fifteen at the time, I loved to be driven in it and indeed be seen to be driven in it, especially whenever I knew a friend might be watching. Dad loved to drive it to its maximum potential whenever he could, and whenever I was sitting in the passenger seat he appeared to be a little more aggressive in his driving technique, as if he was showing off to me for some reason. It must be a macho thing, having to prove something, to your teenage son. I just sat back and let him indulge himself to his little heart's content. I didn't mind one iota. It was great fun.

It was used for almost every occasion. It was employed when he had an important meeting with an accountant or stockbroker, of which there happened to be many around that time, or, to the other extreme, it was taken down narrow country lanes and parked in muddy lay-bys on his ornithological expeditions or "birding trips" as he liked to call them. I kept telling him he should have a Land Rover.

The only trouble with the E-Type was that it took a lot of getting in and out of and I suppose it was this inconvenience that eventually convinced Dad to sell it after eighteen months of ownership. At least he could say that he actually owned an E-Type Jag, and he got it out of his system.

I have touched on earlier the fact that Dad owned three Bristol 400 series cars in quick succession, the 400 (OPJ 6), the 401 (UML 548), and the 405 (WPK 47). These Bristols were first put into production in 1946, so really Dad was one of the first people to own one. I suppose they were the Ferrari of their day and were one of the quickest road cars around, topping 100 mph which was quite a feat at that time.

One motoring journalist of the day wrote, "Buying a Bristol, say those who've had them, is like having your first Savile Row suit made: once you've worn one nothing else will feel quite right."

Dad bought all three from a specialist Bristol dealership called Anthony Crook Motors Limited, in Surrey. Anthony Crook himself was a formula one racing driver of the time with whom Dad struck up a friendship through their love of cars and specifically the Bristol marque. It was through Anthony Crook that Dad also met another racing driver, one Mike Hawthorn, who raced for Ferrari and Jaguar-Bristol on the formula one circuit.

Mike, Dad and Mum met up one lunchtime at a restaurant just outside Brighton, and there was a great deal of friendly banter between Dad and Mike Hawthorn about which was the fastest car, Dad's Bristol 401 or Mike's own highly modified 3.4 litre Jaguar saloon. The argument could never be settled by words alone so they decided to put their respective cars to the ultimate test. A road race. This would not be possible today, but they decided to pick a mutually agreeable coastal route between Brighton and Eastbourne and see which car made the quickest time.

They were actually thinking about racing together but thought better of it and settled for a time trial. The outcome was that the Jaguar made the fastest time but only just. The Bristol 401 was not that far off the pace of Mike's machine. This did not matter one jot to Dad; he had been beaten fairly and squarely by the Jaguar and a racing driver, but it probably dented his pride for some time after.

It was in that very same Jaguar that Mike Hawthorn lost his life in January 1959, racing against a friend's Mercedes on a public road near Guildford in Surrey in similar circumstances to the race against Dad, although this was an impromptu encounter. He was only twenty-nine years old.

Dad was always keen to test out the capabilities

of his beloved Bristol and it was this enthusiasm which got him involved in a spot of rallying. It was not in the premier league of rallying but more of a fun pursuit, albeit a very competitive one. He engaged the help of an old friend from Langton Green by the name of Ernie Sharp as navigator and co-driver and set off to the Welsh mountains to rally the 401. The Bristol looked just the part with the number 359 on a plaque on the front stating the name of the rally and date.

I believe Dad and Ernie more than held their own on this particular Welsh excursion and as always the Bristol created a great deal of attention from spectators and fellow drivers alike. It always surprised me that Dad decided to do this because he was always very fussy about the appearance of his cars, not just the Bristols, but any car he had ever owned. The slightest dirt mark on the bodywork and he was out cleaning it. I remember from a young age watching Dad wash and polish the car of the moment, taking all day if necessary, cleaning in every nook and cranny until it looked as if it had only just been driven out of the showroom.

Sometimes, if he felt so inclined, he would even wash two cars in a day. After a day of rallying in all the conditions the Welsh weather could throw at the Bristol, he must have been up all night bringing it back to concourse condition, only for it to get dirty all over again.

Not all of the cars Dad, and for that matter my mum, owned were glamorous. Mum learned to drive on a red Hillman Husky estate (does anyone actually remember this strange little car?), and after a few lessons managed to reverse the car into a laurel hedge in the garden at Little Pryors. Dad had to call the local garage in Langton to unscrew the chrome bumper to release the car from the hedge. There was a very functional Ford Granada estate which was used from time to time to transport very large boxes of Subbuteo goals to a particular outworker who laboriously fixed the nets onto them. A very fiddly job when there was one or two to do, but imagine having to net up thousands of the so-and-so's.

There was an exceedingly boring white Rover saloon, which was named Ian (EAN). It did not really suit Dad at all, and was more fitted to your local bank manager who would drive it at a very sedate pace, keeping well within the law while wearing nice leather driving gloves and a trilby hat. I have no idea at all what possessed him to buy this car.

Having said that, Dad hardly drove it as he had retained the services of John Scarboro, the proprietor of a Langton-based private car hire firm, to drive the Rover whenever he wanted a trip to London, either on business or pleasure, or to the airport. To all intents and purposes he was Dad's chauffeur, but Dad never referred to him as such, only ever as his driver.

Mind you, he looked every inch the archetypal chauffeur with the beautifully pressed grey suit and leather driving gloves, but minus the peaked cap. Mr Scarboro, as we all called him, never ever John – even Dad – only spoke when he was spoken to while driving, which I always found a little disconcerting. Dad certainly did not insist on this, it was just how

Mr Scarboro liked to conduct himself, like the true professional he was.

I always thought that he looked like Alfred the Butler from the TV series of Batman during the sixties, and I was more often than not told to be quiet and given a sharp slap on the back of the head when he called for us as I started singing, in rather a loud manner, the theme to the Batman programme. If Mr Scarboro ever heard me, he would never had said anything, not even to Dad.

More often than not the chauffeured trips to London were for social reasons rather than on business. Dad, Mum and myself would often be driven up to London in the Rover by Mr Scarboro to have lunch at a top-class West End restaurant, preceded by lunchtime drinks, always at the Ritz Hotel. One of our favourites, or I should say Dad's favourites, was a restaurant called Kettners (now part of the Pizza Express Group – what a shame) in Romilly Street, Soho. Very expensive and frequented by the odd celebrity or two apparently, although I never saw any. Mum once sat opposite the actress Dandy Nichols on one visit. She was the "silly moo" who played Alf Garnett's wife in the sixties comedy series 'Till Death Us Do Part'. Mum kept on about it for weeks after and I'm sure she bored her friends half to tears with that story.

Being driven to London meant, of course, that Dad was able to have a decent drink with his lunch and his favoured tipple at lunchtimes when in London was a bottle of Pouilly Fumé. He imbibed a little too much one particular lunchtime which resulted in a slight impairment of his judgement, or so we thought, when he returned home later in the afternoon. As it turned out it was not the wine; it was Dad being typically Dad, as far as cars were concerned.

Leaving Kettners, he decided to walk off his rather heavy lunch and also to kill some time before he was collected by Mr Scarboro outside the Ritz, where he had been dropped off earlier in the day. Walking along Park Lane, he came across the renowned Rolls Royce dealers, Jack Barclay of Mayfair, and stood for a moment admiring the beautiful machines adorning the showroom window.

He noticed that none of the vehicles on display had a price on them. Presumably, the idea of showing the price, however subtle, was vulgar and anyway if you had to ask the price of a Rolls, the chances were you could not afford one. Without a moment's hesitation Dad strode in, had a quick word with one of the salesmen, emerging a few minutes later with a Rolls Royce brochure tucked under his arm. He had now killed too much time and was in danger of being late for the waiting Mr Scarboro, so he hurriedly made his way back to the Ritz where the Rover was waiting. Mr Scarboro's eyes lit up with anticipation when Dad showed him his newly acquired brochure. But it soon became apparent that Dad had had a few and Mr Scarboro dismissed the brochure as nothing more than a bit of window shopping.

On his arrival home Dad casually threw the brochure in front of Mum, walked away and waited for her reaction. This, of course, was along the lines of, "Don't be so stupid, why on earth would you want a Rolls?" She realised he had had a good lunch and like Mr Scarboro a few hours earlier thought no more of it. Dad was always coming home with car literature, and nine times out of ten nothing ever came of it. But this was to be the tenth time out of ten and it turned out he was deadly serious.

Having mulled over the idea, talked to Mum about it and gone through the literature with a fine toothcomb, he went back to London the following week, this time by train, and, without a trace of alcohol in his blood, strode into the Jack Barclay showroom and ordered a Rolls Royce Silver Shadow, in midnight blue with tan leather upholstery and walnut trim – the works! He paid the required deposit with a balance in the region of £14,000 to pay on delivery in approximately six weeks. This was the late sixties so as you can imagine that was a sizeable amount of money to pay for a car.

For the first few weeks after he had placed his order for the Rolls Dad was on cloud nine, informing a great many of his friends of his purchase and looking forward to the delivery day. As the weeks wore on, somehow doubts started creeping into his head as to whether he had made the right decision in buying a Rolls. Could he actually afford one? Yes, but that wasn't the issue. Was it really and truly his style? Not really. Was it a little pretentious? Most certainly. Could he live with it on a day-to-day basis? Yes, but he didn't want to. Decision made. Much to Mum's relief he contacted Jack Barclay and told them of his decision not to proceed with the sale and would they kindly cancel his order. Apparently, they were very good about it but Dad did lose his deposit, of course. A small price to pay for what could have been a very expensive lack of judgement and taste.

I think it is a fair assumption to make that if it was not for Dad's interest and indeed passion for ornithology, Subbuteo as the famous brand name we all love would never have existed. What a great many people do not realise is that he was interested in and was quite an expert in the field of oology, the study and appreciation of birds' eggs, which is closely linked to ornithology, of course.

He had this knack of being able to tell exactly the breed of bird just by simply looking at the egg, either from an illustration in a book or physically holding it in his hand. It was not only the generic name for the bird he was able to tell, but the subspecies as well. Quite amazing but I suppose if you are interested in a subject you automatically become a fountain of knowledge. He tried to indoctrinate me at a very young age into the complexities of recognising birds and their eggs, buying me books on the subject which I could easily understand and sitting with me for hours poring over these, trying to get my interest. Most children of four or five years of age would be reading Noddy and Big Ears and looking at picture books, not me.

I was being brainwashed into understanding the finer points of the lesser crested grebe and how to spot a marsh warbler from a hundred paces. It was not natural for a child of my age to be studying anything like that. However, although I was not the remotest bit interested in these small birds, much to

Dad's frustration, I did start to take a great deal of interest in birds of prey, of which of course the hobby, or Subbuteo bird, is one. I suppose for a young person these birds have more appeal, being much larger than the average garden bird, and having, as the name implies, a propensity for killing and eating small, or indeed large, rodents and other carrion rather than feeding on insects and berries.

The whole aura of a bird of prey seemed to grab my attention, and it always amazed me how something so big and brutal could look so beautiful and majestic. To this day I am fascinated by these birds. It is the only part of my ornithological upbringing that has stayed with me.

Most weekends as a child were spent with Mum and Dad, being dragged off, most of the time against my will, to go "birding", as we used to call it. Mum was not at all interested really, but I think with her it was a case of "if you can't beat them join them" mentality. We spent hours walking around the local countryside, listening and watching for various types of birds, me armed with a large stick and being encouraged by Dad to poke about in hedges to see if I could spot a bird's nest. His philosophy was that if I was getting involved, instead of just walking and following blindly, some sort of interest in the subject might manifest itself. Wrong. Now, if eagles or vultures nested in the hedges and byways of rural Kent, I would have been well and truly hooked, but unfortunately they don't and I wasn't.

The word 'anorak' is used today for anyone with an obsessive interest and overly detailed knowledge of a particular subject. I might be giving the impression that Dad was an ornithological anorak, but I think that would being doing him an injustice. He would never dream of spending hours talking to people who were just not interested in the subject and inflicting his findings on them. In my opinion that is the fine line between being an anorak and not being one. I may be wrong.

He did, however, spend many hours recording in fine detail the birds he spotted, the birds he heard and also the nests he found and sometimes photographed. All this on top of running Subbuteo to a very high standard of efficiency. It was his safety valve, I guess. To enable him to photograph any nests he found or came across, he always kept in the boot of his car a small set of ladders and a long contractible metal pole with a mirror on the end so he was able to look into nests that were above head height. If he was ever to be stopped by the police and have his car searched, and they came across these particular pieces of equipment, he would have trouble explaining them away as ornithological apparatus. Think about it for one second. A ladder and a long stick with a mirror on the end. People could get the wrong impression.

I don't know whether it was a decision taken to pander to my interest in birds of prey or that Dad was genuinely keen to explore the habitat of the common raven *(corvus corax)* and hopefully photograph a nest, but he had arranged a trip to southern Scotland with a friend of his called John Mullholland and more or less insisted I go with them. Having been on quite a few of Dad's birding trips in the past, and against my will, for once I was quite pleased that I was to be going. The main reason for me being asked was that I was twelve years old and quite lightweight and the idea was that I was probably better physically equipped to climb into rocky crags and get a glimpse of any raven nest we might be lucky enough to encounter. It would have to be an unusually accessible nest as ravens tend to nest very high, beyond the reach of human and other predators. Still, we might get lucky, you never know on these type of expeditions.

As usual with Dad, there was to be no expense spared in kitting me out with the proper gear for this trip and we made a special journey to London's West End to visit the specialist sports equipment shop, Lillywhites of Piccadilly. There I was bought the best pair of leather walking and climbing boots and all the appropriate wet-weather gear that was available. Anyone would think we were going on a polar expedition, not a crag-walking trip in Scotland. Still, it was nice to have all this money spent on me and I enjoyed the thought of looking the part. I insisted on Dad buying me a rucksack to complete the outfit and also the image. All that was needed was a pair of snow goggles.

Dad also bought himself an identical pair of walking boots to mine, but insisted on going to another shop in London for his own outfit to take to Scotland. For some reason, despite having quite suitable attire for the trip, he wanted something new. So we headed straight for a shop he knew quite well, that sold all things, hunting, shooting and fishing, not that we were planning on doing any of those three activities.

Dad disappeared into a cubicle with an armful of clothes he had picked off the rail. He seemed to know the look he was after almost at once and emerged from said cubicle five minutes later wearing a pair of tweed knee-length knickerbockers with contrasting long socks and a matching shooting jacket, complete with poachers' pockets.

All that he needed was a deerstalker hat and that would have been that. I could not believe my eyes and asked Dad to tell me that this was one big joke, but he insisted he was serious and asked the assistant to pack them when he had put his own clothes back on. I kept wondering why on earth he would choose to go to Scotland looking like that when he usually wore normal clothes for his birdwatching trips. He kept threatening me in jest that he would put this outfit on and walk around Tunbridge Wells in it just to get a reaction and wind me up on purpose, but he never did. That's how he was at times, going against the expected. Not eccentric by any stretch of the imagination, but very much his own man.

The trip was planned for my school holidays, and Dad being his own boss at Subbuteo just told everyone he would be off for a week and not to disturb him while he was away. How different to the early days when he felt he needed to oversee every minute of every day.

We made our base in the town of Dumfries, ideally situated for access to the fells and crags to the north of the town. On the first morning, Dad, me and

'Uncle' John started our walk to see if we could spot any ravens. We were pretty confident as this was ideal territory for them. We had been walking for about an hour when high above us we heard a deep 'Brronk' sound, the familiar call of the raven, well, not familiar to me, but to Dad, of course.

This was what we were hoping to hear and kept our eyes peeled on the skies above with the aid of some very expensive and powerful binoculars. Very soon Dad saw an unkindness of ravens circling above. (An *unkindness* is the collective name for a group of ravens).

There must be a nest around the area we thought and so we decided to head for an outcrop of rocks not far away. But to get to it meant negotiating an extremely narrow path with a severe drop on one side. On reaching the path, it was with trepidation that we started to make our way, being wary of each footstep as we were very aware of the long drop beneath us. We could still hear the ravens calling to each other as if they had spotted us encroaching on their territory and were warning us to keep away. The target outcrop was getting nearer and Dad spotted what he thought was a nest on a crag that was jutting out. The drop below was getting steeper as we climbed higher and it was taking all of our concentration to make sure every step taken was a safe one. One false move and, well, it didn't bear thinking about.

At this precise moment I said a few innocent words which would become a family joke for years after. With our lives in the balance on the edge of a sheer 100 foot drop at least, I started rummaging around in my rucksack and shouted the immortal words to Dad and John, "Anyone want a sweetie?"

Dad shouted back something to the effect of just concentrate on where you put your feet and shut up. Back at the hotel that evening we all had a good laugh about it and the incident went down in Adolph folklore as one of the most untimely things ever said in the direst of situations.

Oh, by the way, we did manage to find the ravens' nest and Dad got some magnificent photos, with a little help from me climbing up into areas which would have been impossible for an adult to reach. And thankfully the knickerbockers and shooting jacket saw the light of day only once on the entire trip, much to my relief.

Photography was a passion which, for Dad, could run happily in conjunction with his ornithological pursuits as well as standing as an individual interest on its own merits.

From an early age, he had had an interest in taking photos and not just the run of the mill snapshots taken by most people. There had to be an element of artistic form involved as well. Of course, he took what he liked to call holiday snaps but mainly, even when photographing birds or cars, he was always looking for something special which would set his photo apart from the others.

It was not only the physical aspect of taking and producing a really good shot that he enjoyed: he loved collecting all the equipment that went with it. Lenses, filters, timers, tripods, you name it and he would probably have had one knocking around somewhere, and many of these would be the best and most expensive items you would find.

Names such as Hasselblad, Olympus and, of course, Leica, which is the photographic equivalent of a Porsche. German quality and workmanship again come to the forefront. Some of this equipment looked exceedingly complicated, such as some of the telephoto lenses which needed to be twiddled this way and that to get the correct depth of field and so on and so forth. I don't really understand it myself, but Dad was a real dab hand at using all this complicated equipment. I always pointed out to him that he was able to understand all this business but had no idea how to use a video recorder. It didn't make any sense to me at all.

The best and most interesting piece of photographic equipment he owned was something which would not have been out of place in a James Bond movie. It was a special lens that was able to take photos at a ninety-degree angle, so it would appear that the user was taking a shot directly ahead in the usual way but in fact was focusing on an object in completely the other direction. He bought this for the specific use in Russia, Kiev to be precise, where he went on an expedition in the late seventies. It was to be mainly a birding trip but he was fascinated in capturing the Russian way of life on camera. This involved a great deal of stealth and subterfuge as pointing a camera around at that time, especially on the borders, created a lot of speculation and anxiety among the Russian people. This camera seemed to do the trick and raised no suspicion at all, and he came home with some fantastic shots which would have been impossible to capture had it not been for this unusual piece of equipment.

The results of these Russian photos made him aware that there was much more to photography than just snapping at birds and their nests; that there was a whole world out there just waiting to be captured on camera. He joined the Royal Photographic Society (RPS) based in Bath which has as its slogan, 'Promoting the Art and Science of Photography'. This seemed to appeal to Dad.

His aim was to try his hand at achieving varying levels of distinction in photography, of which there are three, the top being the Fellowship (FRPS), the equivalent of a degree and carrying a vast amount of prestige within the photographic fraternity. Celebrity photographers such as Patrick Lichfield and David Bailey have earned a Fellowship through the RPS, so it was with a great deal of trepidation that Dad decided to start on the first level, the Licentiateship, then progress to the Associateship and finally, if good enough, pass the Fellowship distinction. Each level required the entrant to submit a portfolio of photographs on a chosen subject so there was a theme running through it, and in a format of their choice, for instance, slides, prints or even a video format. This is a basic description of what is required, the reality is a lot more detailed and complicated.

Dad passed his Licentiateship with flying colours which he was obviously chuffed about, and eventually achieved the Associateship after a few tries. He loved the idea of officially being able to put the letters after his name, LRPS and ARPS. However, the Fellowship proved a bridge too far, so he never achieved the highest echelons of photography, despite many, many attempts. He never gave up and was working hard to assemble his umpteenth portfolio for submission to the Fellowship judging panel in 1994 when he passed away. I am sure with his reluctance to give in he would have succeeded in achieving this top status eventually. I would like to think so anyway.

Then of course, there was football in general and Queens Park Rangers FC in particular...

Chapter 6

Real Football

I HAVE ALWAYS been of the strong opinion, still am, that Dad never really took full advantage of his, shall we say, notoriety as inventor of Subbuteo Table Soccer. I know for a cast-iron fact that many professional football clubs, especially during the sixties and the seventies, used Subbuteo to work on tactics during training sessions and also in the changing room prior to and during a match. This would have been an ideal opportunity for Dad to contact any club known to use the game for these purposes and announce who he was and see if he could get some concessions, maybe in the form of a reduced price season ticket or even a complimentary one for that matter.

I was only a youngster at the time but even I could see that there were opportunities there to be had, which not everyone was in a position to take advantage of.

I nagged him and pushed him to at least have a go and see what, if anything at all, was on offer, even if it was targeting one particular club which, of course, would have been Queens Park Rangers. I told him that the worst that could happen would be a polite refusal, but despite my best efforts Dad stood his ground and refused to even entertain the idea. I suppose, looking back, he had his own very good reasons for not wanting to cash in on his brainchild, and I can only think it was his modesty that held him back.

And so it was that he ended up paying the full asking price for two season tickets, one for him and one for me, at Queens Park Rangers during the seventies. We had the same two seats for season after season in the then newly constructed South Africa Road stand. To be fair, they were excellent seats and so they should have been for the price. To be honest, I can't remember the cost but I do know that they were the highest priced seats in the ground and they were three rows from the front of the upper tier in line with the centre circle, and literally within spitting distance of the directors' box. One seat to the left, gangway, directors' box.

Most match days, QPR put on some kind of pre-match entertainment on the pitch, be it the local Shepherds Bush majorettes or a canine football match with some of the little mutts decked out in blue and white hoops with a big red number on their back, being urged on by some dog handler to try unwittingly to emulate their two-legged counter-parts who were by this time locked away in their changing room deep beneath the stand below us, being given a last-minute team talk with tactics courtesy of Subbuteo. If only they knew who was sitting in the stand directly above them.

I remember being not in the slightest way interest-ed in any of this pre-match entertainment, whatever it may have been. The entertainment for me was who I could spot of any fame or notoriety coming to take their seats next to us in the directors' box. It must be pointed out that QPR at this particular time were a top side in the old first division, so many so-called celebrities would come to Loftus Road to watch their football rather than, say, down the road at Fulham or even at Stamford Bridge to see Chelsea who boasted the playing talents of players such as Peter Osgood, Alan Hudson, Charlie Cooke, Dave Webb who was later to become a Ranger, and the not so talented but very effective Ron 'Chopper' Harris.

The normal fare for directors' box occupation on match days were visiting managers of other clubs on a scouting mission, sometimes even the current England manager, with the odd showbiz type thrown in for good measure.

Ironically, during one match I noticed a lanky gentleman sitting two rows directly in front us, wearing a deerstalker hat. He was gesticulating frantically throughout the first half, kicking every ball, making every tackle, saving every shot and ranting and raving at the top of his voice, sometimes not in a very gentlemanly manner. The air was blue with his expletives.

The first half came to an end and the gentleman calmed down immediately, bending forward to pour himself a cup of tea from a thermos he had secreted under his blue plastic seat. He then stood up, lit a cigarette as if to calm his first half-nerves and as he did so I looked down at this now relaxed gentleman and to my surprise realised it was the actor, John Cleese. Basil Fawlty himself, a QPR fan no less. Why was he not in the directors' box? Surely he could have blagged a free ticket. After all, he was arguably one of the highest profile faces on television at the time, what with the current popularity of Fawlty Towers and Monty Python before that. Perhaps he and Dad were of the same persuasion when it came to asking for preferential treatment. We will never know. The times I spent checking the comings and goings to my left and it never ever occurred to me that anyone of any note would be sitting among the common people.

Any football fan will tell you, especially if they have had a season ticket, that sitting in the same seats week in and week out, or to be more precise, fortnight in fortnight out, you do tend to get to know the other fans around you. Occupying the seat next to ours was a lovely old lady, I suppose of around sixty to sixty-five years of age. She always wore the same old, slightly tatty tweed overcoat, and a woolly tea-cosy type of hat on her head and a blue and white QPR scarf worn proudly around her neck, no matter what the weather.

Without fail, she took to her seat a good hour before kick-off and sat there stoically waiting for the game to start, and she always stayed behind at the end of the match to avoid the crowds leaving the stadium. I use the word crowds in the loosest possible sense, because even in those days when the Rangers were doing well, the attendances were never as high as they should have been.

So, this lovely lady was always in her seat when Dad and I arrived at the ground and was still sitting there when we left, and I always had this strange notion that she was a permanent fixture, as if paid by the club to sit there like rent-a-crowd. Both Dad and I were convinced she did not have a home to go to. Anyway, she told us she travelled on her own by coach from Crawley in West Sussex to Shepherds Bush for every home game, and she also went to every away game using the supporters' club coach. She was obviously very well informed on football in general and QPR in particular, and she always gave us an in-depth report on the previous week's away match. I never used to read the newspaper match reports; instead, I waited to hear news of the game direct from the horse's mouth so to speak. She was a real character and a tremendously loyal supporter. I never did find out her name.

This lady occupied a seat on one side of us and a man, who used to travel up from Bournemouth, occupied the seat on the other side. He was an extremely pleasant man to talk to, but as soon as the game was under way he would spend the whole match in total frustration at the way his beloved Rangers were playing. Even when they were playing well and on top of their game, he somehow managed to find fault. No word of praise ever passed his lips.

Dad and I began to wonder why he supported QPR at all and spent so much time travelling to and from the matches. It is a long way to come from Dorset just to be miserable and dejected all afternoon. During one particularly vicious tirade of abuse towards his favoured team, Dad learned over towards him and told him in no uncertain terms that we were all getting a little tired of his rantings and could he possibly keep it down a bit.

He apologised profusely and explained that this was his way of relaxing and unwinding after a hard week of work. It was only at the end of the season that we found out that this man was none other than the well-known author Leslie Thomas, whose most famous novel *The Virgin Soldiers*, was made into a film.

The next home game which would have been at the start of the following season, I took my mum's copy of *The Virgin Soldiers* for him to sign as she was a big fan of all his novels. Dad then proceeded to tell Leslie about the whole Subbuteo connection, which was most out of character, and I do like to think that Mr Thomas went back to Dorset that evening suitably impressed. You never know, Dad might even crop up sometime, albeit in a very roundabout way, in one of Leslie Thomas's novels.

Most of this activity had been happening during the 1975/76 season, when Rangers finished runners-up to Liverpool by one point, and so secured themselves a very lucrative place in the following season's UEFA Cup competition, where they eventually made it to the quarter-final. These were heady days indeed. I have to say that this was beyond doubt the best QPR side Dad or I had ever seen, and suspect it will not be surpassed, not in my lifetime anyway. For the record and for anyone who might be interested, the team was, from one to eleven (no squad numbers in those days): Phil Parkes, Dave Clement, (his son Neil currently plays for West Bromwich Albion), Ian Gillard, John Hollins, Frank McClintock, David Webb, Dave Thomas, Gerry Francis (future England captain), Don Masson, (the great) Stan Bowles and Don Givens, with various substitute appearances by Mick Leach and John Beck.

Stan Bowles was, as far as Dad and I were concerned, undoubtedly the star of the team, but never played for England as much as his talent warranted. Maybe it was his bad boy, gambling playboy image that got in the way or maybe he was just too much of an individual in footballing terms to be accommodated in an England side. Another personal favourite of mine was Dave Thomas, whom Rangers bought from Burnley for £165,000. An orthodox left-winger, who, strangely, was right footed, and he always played tight on the touchline, hardly ever straying infield. I can still hear the crowd as he received the ball, socks always round his ankles, and was off down the touchline at tremendous pace to cross the ball. I remember in one particular match against West Ham he gave their full-back, Frank Lampard, father of current Chelsea and England midfielder Frank junior, a torrid time. He turned him inside out with every foray down the left wing. Such a difficult time in fact that Lampard eventually had to be substituted for his own good. Dave managed to gain only eight England caps over two years, but might have earned more had he been playing for a larger and more glamorous club than QPR.

I have to say that Dad and I never managed to go to as many away matches as we would have liked. We did visit Anfield once to see Rangers play Liverpool, and we were both totally in awe of the place. The atmosphere at Loftus Road was good, or so we thought until we experienced the Kop. There was no comparison. Liverpool FC struck us at the time as being more of a religion than a football club. I'm sure the same still applies today.

We managed a trip to the Baseball Ground, home of Derby County, during the reign of the late, great Brian Clough and Peter Taylor. The journey there started very early one Saturday morning from Eastbourne, where I was at boarding school, and we made it just in time for the three o'clock kick-off. It was a kind of bribe on Dad's part.

He said that if I worked hard at school that term we would go to see this game. Derby was a very big club then so it was one of those 'must see' games, especially with Cloughie at the helm. Despite all his disagreements with the FA, Clough should have undoubtedly been given the chance to manage England at some point in his career. That is an opinion with which many football fans I am sure would agree. A superb managerial talent which should not have slipped through the FA's fingers.

The one away trip which really stood out for me was going to see the Rangers play Manchester United at Old Trafford, again one of those matches during the season that you had to go to watch if possible. We took the train from London on the Friday afternoon, with a room at the Midland Hotel in Manchester already booked. No little bed and breakfast place for Dad. We did these away trips in a little bit of style and the Midland was the best hotel in Manchester, situated in the centre of the city not far from Piccadilly railway station.

On the train journey (first-class, of course, which to my mind was a complete waste of money because you didn't get there any quicker, you just got a bit more room and privacy), we decided to venture to the buffet car to partake of some light afternoon refreshment, which is a genteel way of saying a cuppa and a slab of dry British Rail cake. The buffet car was quite empty at the time so we had no trouble in finding a table, and we were both tucking in to the aforementioned tea and cake when, and I still can't quite believe it even now, the entire QPR first team came in.

I had just finished nudging Dad to make him aware of their presence, when a voice in a thick north-eastern accent said, "mMind if I sit 'ere? " To my surprise and amazement it was Dave Thomas. *The* Dave Thomas. The man who I had been watching week in and week out flying down the wing at Loftus Road.

He sat opposite us with his polystyrene cup of coffee, gave it a quick stir and proceeded to look casually out of the buffet-car window. After a short while he started to make polite conversation and Dad told him we were QPR fans on our way to Manchester for the match the following day. I was totally star-struck at meeting one of my football heroes. I actually hate the word, 'hero' being used in connection with sportsmen and women as I feel it undermines the true meaning of the word and should only really be used for those people who deserve it. After all, they do not save lives or have ever fought for their country. The bottom line is that they are entertainers and that is all.

OK, climbing down off the proverbial soapbox now, I got myself so excited at meeting one of my favourite players that with one swipe of my hand, I accidentally knocked my entire cup of tea over the table and over Dave Thomas. It went everywhere, as a relatively small amount of liquid tends to do. His smart blue club suit was totally saturated.

I offered my profuse apologies as he mopped himself down with a load of paper napkins that Dad had rushed to find from the bar. I just wanted the ground to open up and swallow me whole. He was very understanding and just laughed off the whole incident, saying that accidents happened. Dad, on the other hand, was not as forgiving and had a right go at me for me being so clumsy and there was an atmosphere between us you could have cut with a knife until we reached Manchester.

We wished Dave good luck for the forthcoming match and took our leave swiftly from the buffet car. Most people when they meet their idols ask for their autograph. Not me. I just deposit a cup of boiling hot liquid in their lap. What a way to show your appreciation.

We settled into our room at the Midland Hotel with the whole tea saga still going through my mind. But at least Dad had calmed down and we were talking again. We thought we had better find out how far away we were from Old Trafford and the best way to get there from the hotel. Dad said that he was going down to the hotel reception to do some investigation and did I want to come with him or stay in the room?

I said I would stay put and read some magazines I had brought with me and off Dad went downstairs. I checked the clock as Dad left and it was six o'clock. Soon be time for a nice hotel meal, I thought as my stomach started to rumble. In all the chaos that had happened on the way up in the buffet I had completely forgotten to eat my slab of British Rail cake.

I woke up with a start and wondered for a fleeting second where I was and what I was doing in this hotel bedroom. I must have dozed off for a second. I glanced at the clock, and to my horror it certainly was more than a second, for the clock now told me it was eight-fifteen. Where was Dad? He had only popped down to reception to sort out the travel to Old Trafford. There was no way it would have taken him more than two hours to do that. I went to the door, opened it and looked down the long corridor to the lifts to see if I could see him.

There was no one around, except a couple of chambermaids going about their evening duties, so I went back into the room, put on my shoes and decided to investigate and perhaps ask at reception to ascertain if indeed Dad had been down a few hours ago to get some information, and did they know where he had gone. The receptionist informed me that, yes, Mr Adolph had been making enquiries a few hours before and that as far as she could remember he left the hotel immediately afterwards.

I have to admit to a sense of creeping panic on hearing this information and decided to go outside to look around. Nothing. Now all kinds of negative thoughts were running through my head, as you might imagine. I headed back into the hotel and sat down in the lounge to gather myself. I was just about to get up and go back to the room when a distinctly slurred voice from behind me said, "Sorry, Mark, I thought I would just pop out and investigate the local hostelry."

It was Dad, rather the worse for alcohol, but still able to speak and walk, after a fashion. The clock behind the reception desk showed eight forty-five. Too relieved to be angry with him, I took him by the arm, said my thank yous to the receptionist and escorted him back to our room, where he promptly flopped onto the bed and fell fast asleep. Bang went my nice hotel meal, and I went to sleep with my stomach still rumbling. It was a competition that night between Dad's snoring and my grumbling stomach.

Next morning, Dad was surprisingly chirpy and tucked into a really hearty breakfast in the hotel restaurant. He never, ever appeared to suffer any sort of hangover, and so I thought I had better broach the subject of what actually happened the previous evening. Apparently, he had found a pub a few hundred yards away from the hotel, intending only to have a swift gin and tonic. But he got chatting with a few people. It transpired they were from Stoke and were in town for the Port Vale match the next day at neighbouring Stockport County.

Somehow, Dad had mentioned the Subbuteo thing in conversation, which he used to do only with a couple of beverages inside him, and it transpired that many of these Port Vale fans were also huge Subbuteo fans. They insisted that he stayed for one more drink, and then one more and so on. All the time Dad insisted he had to return to his hotel where his son was waiting for him.

It was later when we returned to the hotel room that Dad found, stuffed in the pocket of the jacket he had been wearing the previous evening, a black and white Port Vale scarf, with the words 'Pride of the Potteries' emblazoned on it and I accepted his story completely.

Lunchtime came, and acting on the information given to him the previous evening, before his encounter with the lads from the Potteries, Dad and I headed for the nearby bus station to catch our bus to Old Trafford for the three o'clock kick-off. As usual, I was decked out with my customary QPR scarves, a woolly one and a silk one – I called it silk but of course it was a horrible nylon, polyester concoction, with the highly original 'Pride of London' written on it. Pride of London, Pride of the Potteries – who thinks up these slogans?

Pinned to my jacket was a blue and white rosette. That jacket. I think back now to this particular day and squirm at what I was wearing. To be honest, I think I was a little self-conscious at that time. Wearing this outfit in and around Tunbridge Wells would have been bad enough, but to wear it to a football match, and not just any old football match, a match at Old Trafford, the home of the mighty Manchester United, was a mistake of gargantuan proportions. I recall mentioning to Dad that I felt inappropriately dressed for the occasion and all he could say in a very fatherly way was how smart I looked.

I didn't want to be smart at all. I wanted to feel that I fitted in and not stand out like a sore thumb. It was a sky-blue jacket, in the style of a shirt but worn open with a flower-patterned shirt underneath, with matching blue, very flared trousers. If it had been denim it would have been fairly acceptable, but it was made of a very shiny cotton material. Horrendous.

We got off the bus a short walk away from Old Trafford and made our way to the ground, surrounded by masses of United fans, many of whom were in Doc Martins, half-mast jeans, braces and skinhead haircuts, with tartan scarves tied around their wrists, which was *de rigueur* for Man U fans at the time due to the high number of Scottish players in their ranks. We eventually made the rather uncomfortable short journey from bus to stadium and settled ourselves in our seats, ready for the big kick-off.

Four forty-five came and we had lost to the mighty Manchester United. Leaving the ground, I could not help feeling partly responsible for our loss. Had I unwittingly sabotaged our own winger with the hot tea incident almost twenty-four hours earlier? Surely not.

The return fixture against Manchester United at Loftus Road later on in the season was equally eventful but for very different reasons. Gone were the horrific blue suit and flowery shirt, replaced with something a little more in keeping for attending a football match. It was something midway between bovver boy and catalogue man, I suppose. Of course, it was a full house at Shepherds Bush this time and everyone was full of anticipation, hoping to even things up after the defeat at Old Trafford.

We got a full match report as usual on our previous away match at Everton from our lovely old lady from Crawley, and Leslie Thomas arrived very late following the delay of his train up from Bournemouth. It was a cracking match with a wonderful atmosphere and we won 3-1. Dad and I were totally elated.

Any win was heralded as a major triumph, but a win against Manchester United was an added bonus. To this day, if anyone asks me which team I support, I always say, tongue in cheek, that it is any team playing Manchester United. Leaving our seats after the match was the usual slow affair, but before we could climb down the stairs to street level, there was a delay while the police escorted an enormous throng of Man U fans past our side of the ground. There was a lot of banter between us, the QPR fans in the stand, and the United fans being herded along South Africa Road below us. I was waving my scarf at them in a very provocative manner, and receiving a lot of abuse back, but I felt safe doing this, being high up in the stand among my own kind.

The travelling support was eventually cleared by the police and Dad and I continued to make our way back to the car which was parked as usual in a typical West London street of terraced houses, about ten minutes' walk from the ground. We knew the maze of streets like the back of our hand. We were very nearly at the car so I stole a march on Dad who was about thirty feet behind. I was keen to listen to the football results on the car radio. I had just turned into the street where the car was parked when from nowhere two lads appeared and ran at me from across the road, one pushing me hard against a wall in front of a house, while the other punched me hard in the stomach.

I was winded but managed to make out that each of them had Manchester United scarves tied around their wrists. The lad who had pushed me initially was just about to administer a second punch when Dad appeared from around the corner and ran to my assistance, shouting at them to leave me alone. He didn't say it as politely as that but you get the idea.

When Dad reached the scene, one of lads turned on him and headbutted him in the mouth. They then disappeared as quickly as they had appeared. All this happened in a minute but, as always in these situations, it seemed to go on for ever. Dad asked if I was OK and I told him I was although a little shaken.

Dad had a great deal of blood around his mouth, which was running down his chin and onto his jacket. We got into the car and Dad examined himself in the rear-view mirror, discovering his lip was very badly gashed, worse than he had anticipated. He cleaned himself up as best as he could with tissues he found in the boot, trying to stem the flow of blood. We sat there, both a little shocked, and decided what to do next.

Obviously, Dad needed his lip looked at as soon as possible as it was still pouring blood at a tremendous rate, but we decided to go and report the incident to the police straight away.

Not that we thought it would do any good as the culprits would be well away by now, but still we made our way to the police station in Shepherds Bush, about half a mile away on the Uxbridge Road. We passed it on every trip up to see the Rangers, never thinking that we would ever have cause to pay a visit. Luckily, the car was an automatic so Dad managed to drive there, one hand steering and the other holding a tissue to his damaged mouth. The blood was thankfully easing off by now.

The police went through the usual procedures, telling us that we were correct in reporting the incident, but that they were unfortunately unable to do anything to apprehend the perpetrators, despite us giving them as good a description of them as we could. It was all red tape. I'm sure this was a run of the mill procedure for them, especially on a match day at Loftus Road. Having spent the best part of an hour at the police station, Dad's lip had now stopped bleeding, but it did look very swollen and so we thought it best if we stopped off at the Charing Cross Hospital, which happened to be on our way home, to have it looked at, rather than wait until we got back to Tunbridge Wells.

The wait at Accident and Emergency was not too long, and Dad was seen quite quickly which was a bonus. We emerged an hour later with Dad having needed five stitches to his upper lip and me being given the all-clear despite a bad headache and a very sore abdomen. Dad came off worse coming to my rescue and I remember feeling so guilty about that. If only I hadn't carried on ahead in my urgency to hear the football results on the car radio. If only I hadn't been so exuberant in my victory celebrations up in the stand. Maybe I was recognised from all those QPR fans and singled out and followed by those two United thugs. If only I had been a little more aware of what I was doing. My mind was running riot with the guilt. Dad was fine about it and told me not to be so hard on myself and, if the truth be known, I do believe he felt a bit of a hero.

Tonbridge FC, with all the respect in the world, is hardly a name to set the pulse racing in football circles. The West Kent side played in what was called the Southern League in the late sixties and early seventies, an amateur league probably some ten or so divisions off the old first division. Their ground was the usual ramshackle affair one normally associates with clubs of that stature. A covered area, with four or five tiers of terracing along one side of the pitch, and the main stand, with wooden seating housing the directors' box, at one end of the ground behind the goal, with the other two sides of the ground open to the elements and also to anyone not honest enough to pay at the turnstiles. The average attendance would probably have been a couple of hundred if they were lucky and more than likely a lot less if they were playing on a wet Tuesday evening in November.

It was against this backdrop of a typical amateur league football club that Dad was approached by Tonbridge FC to become their honorary vice-chairman. It was a position he had to think about as he was a little bit suspicious about why he was being asked. But he came to the conclusion he was being a bit too sensitive and it was an honour to be asked so he graciously accepted their kind and indeed flattering invitation.

I suppose the club thought that having 'Mr Subbuteo' on board would be good for their image and add a touch of local interest and prestige, and who knows, even bring a few more local people through the turnstiles. Mind you, at the time Dad joined the club, one of their directors was none other than George Cohen, the 1966 England World Cup winning full-back, who lived in the Tunbridge Wells area. How much more prestige did this little club want?

It was at this time that we were going to Shepherds Bush to watch QPR and as luck would have it, or thinking about it, perhaps not, the Rangers' away fixtures coincided with Tonbridge's home matches, so in effect Dad and I were going to a match every Saturday, and sometimes midweek as well. Suffice to say that the standard and quality of football witnessed at Tonbridge fell somewhat short of that which we enjoyed in London. We would sit in our seats in the directors' box at Tonbridge and secretly cringe at the quality of football to which we were being subjected. Dad always used to comment, on the quiet of course, that watching Tonbridge was akin to watching school kids playing football in the playground. There appeared to be no discernible system of playing or indeed tactics, just kick and rush as he liked to call it.

One week we would be witnessing the grace, artistry and skill of Stan Bowles and the following week some plumber or builder plying his footballing trade on a Kentish mudbath. Dad, of course, had to make all the right noises to his counterparts on the board of directors during the game, marvelling at the silky skills employed by the new midfield dynamo bought for the price of a few tracksuits and a crate of local beer from local rivals Hastings United or some such equally awful amateur club. The fact of the matter was that this new signing was no more than a clogger and even a crate of beer was too big a transfer fee.

It might seem I am doing down the quality of football at this level, but really I am not. To be fair, taking the whole standard on its own merits it was not too bad. It is when one compares it with top-flight football that one can become a tiny bit cynical. Surprisingly enough, halfway through Dad's first season as vice-chairman, the club were lying in fifth spot, a few places off promotion and things were looking up on the pitch.

But there was no apparent rise in spectator numbers and hence no increase in revenue which the club desperately needed. There was no shirt sponsorship then and although there was space for advertising on the hoardings around the perimeter of the pitch, not many of the local firms were prepared to fork out to have their name emblazoned on them. I do believe at some point it was mooted that Dad should shell out and advertise Subbuteo, but I think any approaches made to Dad by the chairman fell on deaf ears, and so the subject was swiftly dropped and never mentioned again.

Dad was always very sensitive to the fact that he personally, and also the name Subbuteo, could be taken advantage of, hence his initial reluctance to join the club as vice-chairman.

Into the second half of the season the club seemed to be holding their own in the higher echelons of the Southern League, and as it progressed it seemed that they might secure a promotion place, provided they could improve on their away form. They started picking up a few points away, just at the right time, and consolidated their home form which was fairly consistent despite the obvious lack of support. With three games to go, Tonbridge FC were in third place and needed to secure at least two wins to guarantee promotion in second place. The stumbling block was that two of the three games were away, with what could be the decider at home in the last game.

Tensions were running high as Dad and I took our seats in the directors' box for the final game which was against Dorchester Town. The club had won one and lost one of their two previous games away, so nothing less than a win would give them promotion.

Dad and I noticed that despite this being a do-or-die match, the crowd was not as big as it should have been for a game of this magnitude. A fact that did not go unnoticed by the other directors and board members sitting in the directors' box. If promotion was achieved, surely playing football at a higher level would bring in the punters in their droves. Only time would tell. Ninety minutes to be precise.

The first forty-five minutes saw a very tense affair with Tonbridge playing very edgily with neither side managing to break the deadlock. Nil-nil at half-time.

The manager must have read the team the riot act at half-time, for they came out for the second half full of confidence with the real belief that they could win. Whatever means of motivation the manager used had an immediate effect, as the first corner of the second half in Tonbridge's favour, was nodded home by their lanky centre-half. I cannot recall his name but I do seem to remember he was once on the books of Crystal Palace, but failed to make the grade at Selhurst Park.

That was the only goal of the game and when the final whistle went the place erupted and everyone in the directors' box hugged each other. They were up. Although pleased the club had achieved promotion in his first season of involvement, I got the distinct impression from Dad that something was playing on his mind. I knew how his mind worked and I was sure that everyone would find out more at a later date.

After the celebrations in the stand, Dad, along with his chairman and directors, was summoned to the players' changing room to administer words of congratulations and to be soaked with the customary champagne, although in this particular case I believe it was more likely to be fizzy wine or even a vigorously shaken can of Best Bitter.

Dad was asked to say a few words to the victorious team, most of whom gathered around to hear what 'Mr Subbuteo' had to say. Dad was most definitely not at ease standing up to say his piece, but he got through it all right and I think that everyone appreciated what he had to say. Everyone had a good evening and Dad was just about to say his farewells and head for home when he was apprehended by the chairman, who suggested to him that they have an informal meeting together, just the two of them, to discuss plans for the following season. Dad agreed and said he would phone in the next few days to arrange this meeting.

The next morning, with the promotion celebrations over, the full consequences of a successful season soon became blindingly apparent to Dad. The team would need to be strengthened to enable them to compete as successfully as possible at a higher level, which obviously meant signing new players, but not the ones who could be bought for a couple of tracksuits. The best players were available for hard cash only, and this was a commodity the club lacked. So where was this money going to be coming from? You have guessed it. And so did Dad. He promptly phoned the chairman and resigned with immediate effect as vice-chairman of Tonbridge FC, after only one, albeit rather successful, season on board. Personal team building should be left to Russian oil billionaires only.

Tonbridge FC is still in existence today, but now are known by the rather Americanised name of the Tonbridge Angels. The ramshackle ground was sold not long after Dad resigned, to be replaced by a large supermarket complex, the one where 'good food costs less'. The Angels are currently playing in the Ryman League Division One and have a new stadium in the town. Very occasionally, the Tonbridge Angels' score come up on Gillette Soccer Saturday, on Sky Sports, and I always have a feeling of pride that Dad was once vice-chairman of this little club.

Chapter 7

Subbuteo Abroad – Business and Pleasure

THE FIRST PRODUCTION of Subbuteo abroad came in 1963, firstly in Gibraltar followed very quickly by a production operation in Barcelona. It was run by George Erik and traded under the name of Aquila, yet another example of Dad using the Latin names of birds for his companies. This was the Latin for Eagle.

Erik, as he was known to everyone, was one of life's great characters, a stage-set designer by trade, but he could turn his hand to model-making and a very good job he made of it too. He was also an aficionado of the bullfight, an all-round expert, which coming from an Englishman was rather hard for the Spaniards, who had bullfighting in their blood, to understand. It was Erik who first introduced me to the magic of the bullfight as a spectacle.

The Gibraltar and Barcelona operations were run on a similar basis to the one in Langton Green, with the figures being moulded and then farmed out to local outworkers for the hand-painting process before being shipped to England for assembly. At its height Barcelona was sending back more than one hundred thousand painted Subbuteo figures per week, with Gibraltar sending back around twenty thousand,

and all this in addition to the figures being produced in Kent.

It was a massive and worthwhile operation but it did need Dad to make many trips to both Gibraltar and Barcelona to oversee the whole thing, although Erik was the main man in Spain. Dad realised that if he could combine trips abroad with birdwatching, it would be beneficial for all concerned and it was with this in mind that he eventually bought an apartment in Gibraltar as a base for both business and pleasure, paid for by Subbuteo, of course. It was a lovely apartment, of typical Mediterranean design, overlooking Gibraltar's harbour and marina, and aptly named Marina Court. This would also become a secret retreat to which he and Mrs Z would go to spend a bit of time away from England. To outsiders it was Dad and his secretary away on business, but on closer examination it was more than that although even the Subbuteo staff on the Rock and the outworkers never suspected a thing.

The post-World Cup era for Subbuteo was one of the high points in the game's history, and as far as our family were concerned, I suppose it was also the most decadent of times as well. There was certainly no shortage of money and I would think it would be the nearest the three of us ever came to having a jet-set lifestyle. Although I detest that phrase, it does encapsulate what life was like around this time, but on my part it is only in retrospect that I have come to appreciate how lucky I was to have and experience the things I did.

Dad bought his suits from Savile Row, his shirts

from Jermyn Street, and all his shoes were handmade in leather. Mum bought most of her clothes from Aquascutum in Bond Street and from Jaeger, and although she was not that fond of flashy jewellery, she did treat herself to an enormous diamond ring from a small independent jeweller's in Brighton, which she wore on a daily basis despite its size and value. If anyone commented on how beautiful her ring was, she would always joke that it was amazing what Woolworths sell nowadays. That was typical of her humour and wanting to appear not too over the top.

As with a good many people living in England having to endure seemingly endless winters, by the time the Christmas and New Year festivities had come to an end we were fed up with the cold and gloomy weather. We were fortunate enough to be able to jet off in search of winter sunshine and for many years, at the start of January, our destination of choice was Cannes in the South of France for a week or ten days. We flew first-class by Air France (or Air Chance as we sometimes called it whenever our flight happened to be delayed) to Nice and hired a car to drive along the French Riviera to Cannes, where we stayed in the five-star Hotel Majestic situated on the famous Croissette strip, the seafront overlooking the town's harbour with its array of exclusive private yachts anchored for the winter.

The January sunshine on the Riviera was beautiful, reaching temperatures around the mid-sixties, which is what we might expect on a pleasant May day in England. It was not unusual for Dad to venture into the hills behind Cannes on one of his birding trips and leave Mum and I to enjoy the facilities at the hotel, which included swimming in the beautiful kidney-shaped outdoor pool. Swimming in January was a real treat and it made us glad that we were where we were and not shivering by the fireside in England, waiting in earnest for the onset of spring.

On a couple of occasions, Dad invited my good friend Richard to come with us on these post-Christmas trips to Cannes, which was great for me as it meant I had someone of my own age with whom to enjoy the whole experience. We were about twelve, and of course Richard was my most regular Subbuteo opponent. On one trip, so as not to be deprived of our one consuming passion for too long, we took along a Subbuteo pitch and a few teams and set up our matches in the hotel room, much to Dad's annoyance as he quite rightly pointed out that he had spent all this money coming to the South of France to stay in a lovely hotel and we were holed up in our room playing Subbuteo which we could have been doing at home for nothing. It was a fair enough point.

I think a few members of the hotel staff must have seen our games set up in the room when they came on their daily rounds to clean the rooms, and, putting two and two together, the word soon got round that Mr Subbuteo was a guest at their establishment. It was surprising how many people approached Dad in the bar and the restaurant wanting to chat about the game and regale him with their Subbuteo experiences, most of them in French, of course. Dad got the gist of it as his French was not too bad, but a few spoke in very broken English which was harder to understand. I think one of the waiters wanted Dad to have a game with him, but he politely refused saying that he was on a break and to be honest wanted to get away from it all for a while.

It was on one of these trips with Richard that we experienced for the first time what really went on after dark even in the most exclusive parts of the world. Being so young this was quite an eye-opener for me and I am sure it was for Richard as well.

Mum and Dad were taking us for an evening meal at a restaurant a few hundred yards along the Croissette from our hotel and we were walking a short distance in front of them, larking around and behaving like boys of our age would do, when, from the shadows of a shop doorway, two 'ladies of the night' stepped forward and starting chatting with us, in French quite naturally. Neither of us could understand what they were saying nor did we realise what they were. As far as we were concerned they were just being friendly.

Mum and Dad saw what was going on and found it strange that these ladies would take the time to stop and attempt to solicit business from boys of our age. It was only on our return walk back to the hotel that I spotted these ladies again and pointed them out that Dad realised that in fact they were not of the female persuasion at all but were very convincing transvestites, chatting up a couple of young boys. When we had thought they were females we laughed about the absurdity of the situation, but on realising that they were a couple of ladyboys it made our stomachs turn to think that it was not as innocent as wehad first thought. Having said that, it was something we all looked back on in later years and had a good giggle about.

The Cunard cruise liner *Queen Elizabeth 2 (QE2)* was launched in September 1969, and her maiden voyage on 2nd May 1969 from Southampton to New York, made quite an impact on the world's media, and it certainly made an impression on Dad. He always had a compulsion to sample the latest and most up-to-date innovations that came onto the market, be it the humblest music system or television, to the latest model of car that took his fancy.

Seeing this magnificent ship on the television leaving Southampton for a six-day trip to New York whetted his appetite to cruise on it in its very early days. He mentioned very casually one day that he would quite fancy a trip on the *QE2* and how did Mum and I feel about booking a transatlantic cruise to New York, staying in the Big Apple for a few days and then flying back? We didn't have to think twice and accepted straight away, and again in typical style, Dad decided that if it was to be done, it was to be done in the best possible manner. He booked us all on the *QE2* in first-class accommodation, for a July departure, booked one of the best hotels in New York, the Pierre on Central Park, and first-class airline tickets home. There was no way this trip of a lifetime was to be done on a budget.

July eventually arrived and I had been looking forward to the trip since the day it had been booked in May. It may not have been the maiden voyage we were going on, but it was certainly the second or third transatlantic trip the *QE2* was undertaking so it was quite a journey to make. On boarding, it struck me at once how vast the ship was and it took a while to grasp the fact that this was a brand-new vessel, and how relatively few people had sailed in her, and here we were making our way to our first-class cabins on the upper decks.

Opulence is a word that springs to mind in describing our two adjacent cabins. Thick pile carpet throughout, with fantastically comfortable beds. Décor in the finest possible taste, with gold-plated taps in the ensuite bathrooms. All mod cons in fact, and so it should have been for the price although I don't recall exactly how much the whole trip cost Dad in total, but it was a tidy sum, of that there is no doubt.

It took a day or so to find your bearings on board and to find the quickest routes so by the time everything was familiar, it was time to leave the ship. It was that huge, this floating hotel. After the initial buzz of being on board and the fun in exploring the whole ship, I have to admit to suddenly finding the whole experience a bit boring. Despite its size, I had this feeling of being trapped and having to socialise with people I would not necessarily choose to be with had I been anywhere else but on a ship. I was encouraged to attend the many activities that were put on specifically for youngsters of my age, like discos and film shows and swimming galas and that kind of thing, but I just did not want to know, much to Dad's annoyance. He kept reminding me of how much this experience had cost him and that I was to bloody well muck in and try to enjoy myself. This had the opposite effect and I dug in my heels even more and eventually Dad reluctantly left me alone to do what I wanted.

Things started getting a little more interesting for me when halfway across the Atlantic we encountered the very outer edge of a hurricane, which despite making the sea appear as calm as a millpond, actually created an enormous swell beneath the surface which threw all 70,000 tons of cruise liner around like a toy boat. It had the effect of confining eighty per cent of the ship's passengers to their cabins with severe seasickness for twenty-four hours including Mum and me. Dad, on the other hand, having a cast-iron stomach, was more than happy to carry on regardless, venturing onto the upper decks to take in the whole experience.

He even managed to carry on eating as normal, whereas for the rest us mortals just the thought of even the tastiest morsel sent us retching to the nearest available bathroom. I'm convinced Dad thought that anyone not behaving normally was a little on the precious side, but the truth is he was in the minority, carrying on as if touching the edge of a hurricane was an everyday happening.

After six days of being on the high seas, I for one was pleased to disembark in New York and feel the security of solid ground beneath my feet, but for a day I was still in possession of my sea legs and had the feeling of a lurching ship beneath me. Most odd.

It had taken an age to get off the *QE2* even

though being first-class passengers we had priority to disembark first, so it must have appeared like a lifetime for those not as fortunate as us. We hired a taxi to take us to the hotel, and the route there took us into Wall Street, the famous financial district of New York City. We encountered a street strewn with what we soon found out to be tickertape thrown from the offices which lined the street.

On enquiring from the taxi driver what all this tickertape was in aid of, we were told that we had missed, by only a couple of hours, the parade through the streets of New York and a tickertape welcome for the Apollo 11 astronauts, Neil Armstrong, Buzz Aldrin and Michael Collins, who had splashed down on July 24th after their historic trip to the moon and Armstrong and Aldrin's moonwalk.

We did not have that long in New York, certainly not long enough to really appreciate this fantastic city, but we did manage to take in the usual tourist attractions like the Empire State Building and the Statue of Liberty, which by the way was an awesome sight when we approached it on the *QE2*, surrounded by the early morning mist.

After three days taking in all we could in New York, we caught our VC10 flight back to England. It is certainly an experience I have always remembered. I look back on these voyages and the many post-Christmas weeks in Cannes and think that if it wasn't for those little plastic footballers, none of it would have been possible – not in the style we did it anyway.

Trips to Barcelona were to become more and more

frequent for Dad and on many occasions Mum and I would accompany him. We would always stay at the same five-star hotel, the Avenida Palace, located in the centre of this magnificent city only a few minutes' walk from the famous Las Ramblas avenue and the harbour area of the city. Las Ramblas was a vibrant place, especially at night, with its pavement cafés, restaurants and street entertainers, which comprised mainly tacky flamenco dancing shows aimed purely at the tourist market. If you wanted to witness real flamenco for the indigenous Spanish population, you would have to negotiate the narrow, slightly seedy back streets which ran like a rabbit warren adjacent to Las Ramblas. In these flamenco clubs you find only the true enthusiasts of this ancient and traditional form of Spanish dance, not the two-week Spanish holiday Brit, craving to see a piece of real Spanish culture.

I am sure flamenco was not the only entertainment on offer, if you knew the right people or indeed the proprietor. One of these flamenco clubs, which went by the name of Los Tarantos, was frequented by Dad a great many times during his numerous trips to Barcelona. It was one of those places that you could go to indulge in some extremely late-night drinking and was well away from the tourist trap of Las Ramblas. It was at Los Tarantos that another avenue of intrigue was soon to be opened for Dad.

The Avenida Palace Hotel, I have to say, was probably the best and the most opulent hotel I ever stayed in, and I had stayed in quite a few top-notch places during my trips abroad with Mum and Dad, all paid for by Subbuteo of course. The staff at the Avenida soon got to know Dad really well over the years and on his arrival the doorman would greet him with a friendly, "Buenos dias, senõr Adolph," and escort him and his luggage to the front reception desk, where an equally warm welcome awaited him from the duty manager behind the counter. They knew exactly the type of room he wanted and nine times out of ten he always had the same, whether he had the family in tow or was on his own.

I say room, but it was actually a suite, with a sitting-room area and double doors leading into the master bedroom, which in turn led to a hallway, and off that was the most magnificent bathroom you could imagine with all the mod cons. The hallway boasted a minibar, which at that time was quite a luxury, although nowadays they are taken for granted even in run of mill motels. The said minibar was hit hard most days and then refilled again in a self-perpetuating round of alcohol.

In the hallway next to the front door to the suite, situated a few inches above floor level, was a tiny louvred door, about the size of a cat flap. It never failed to intrigue me as to what this was for, and I used to spend many an hour sitting on the floor just opening and shutting this tiny wooden door, secretly spying on any guest as they walked past our suite in the corridor outside, much to the annoyance of Mum and Dad, who told me to stop doing that, to grow up and do something constructive.

Fair point, I suppose, but it was really just a case of doing anything except what I was supposed to be doing, which was the schoolwork I was made to bring with me on these trips, so I did not fall behind during the long school holidays. Dad especially was a bit of a hard taskmaster as far as schoolwork was concerned and I really resented taking it with me. I was supposed to be on holiday for Christ's sake. I always wondered if any of my school chums were made to take work away with them. I convinced myself that I was the only one in the whole school whose parents were so mean and insistent on schoolwork in the holidays that it made me stick to my low-level lookout post onto the corridor even more.

It transpired that this little wooden door served a very specific purpose. The hotel operated a shoe-cleaning service during the night and the idea was that guests left their shoes outside their rooms at night before retiring. They were collected and cleaned while you were asleep and returned to you in the morning by the hotel staff who opened the little wooden door and deposited your shiny shoes onto the floor of your room. A brilliant service but it left itself wide open to abuse by anybody with half a mind to send the whole system into meltdown. And that 'anybody' on one occasion was Mum.

Dad had received a phone call from Erik saying he had arranged, at very short notice, a meeting at a local bar with some of the Subbuteo staff in Barcelona to iron out a few production problems which had been going on for a while now, and thought that Dad's presence in town might help to alleviate and solve these gremlins in the otherwise smooth-running Spanish Subbuteo machine. Erik, like Dad, always tried to do any business in a bar with a few alcoholic beverages, rather than going down the more formal route of meeting in the office.

Mum decided that she and Erik's wife Barbara would go to the meeting so they could get together for some girlie chat and a few Subbuteo-bought drinks. I had the choice to accompany them to this meeting, but I decided I wanted to stay in the hotel, so Dad had room service deliver my evening meal which was a fantastic experience for someone so young. A whole evening to myself in a luxurious hotel suite. I remember wondering what my friends back in England would have made of this. I'm sure they would have been green with envy.

I had the television on in the room, hoping I might find a channel that was showing a football match and maybe it might even be Barcelona playing at the Nou Camp Stadium. All I could find was a programme similar to our 'Match of the Day' showing highlights of a very poor Spanish second division game. The programme was just coming to an end when, coming from the corridor outside our room, I heard screaming and laughing from what sounded like a few very drunk women, running up and down outside. I went to the hall and looked through our little spy door and was shocked to see it was Mum and Barbara a little worse for wear after what I presumed was a very successful meeting with Erik and the Subbuteo staff.

They ran back towards our room, with Mum making a complete meal of the simple task of opening the door with her key. She decided to give up and shouted and banged on the door for me to let her and Barbara in, and they then both fell into the room trying hard not to let it show that they had had a few too many drinks. I had already gathered this was the case and told them that I had seen them behaving like idiots running up and down the corridor. I enquired politely what they had been up to. I was immediately told to mind my own business, as they headed towards the minibar to see what was on offer. I knew they had been up to something untoward but it was not until the next morning that all was to be divulged.

In their drunken state, they had both gone methodically along the corridor swapping around the shoes that had been left outside for their nightly shoeshine, so in the morning guests were getting back other people's shoes through their little wooden doors. It sounds very juvenile, but looking back, I suppose it was rather amusing. Obviously, numerous complaints were made at reception but I don't think that the hotel staff managed to trace this misdemeanour back to the Adolph suite. Even if they had, Dad was a good customer so I would imagine not a great deal would have been said.

Both Mum and Dad were a bit fragile the next day, but Dad had managed to sort out the Subbuteo problem with Erik and there was to be no fallout regarding the unfortunate shoe incident, so all was well. Whenever we were in Barcelona we always tried to get to see a bullfight or *La Corrida*, as the Spanish call it. Now I do realise that there is a great deal of controversy regarding this particular, shall we say, 'sport' (or is it an art form?) and this is not exactly the correct medium to go into the pros and cons of this highly emotive subject, but I have to say that as a spectacle it is a truly magnificent sight to behold. The atmosphere is always electric and, rightly or wrongly, I became hooked on this uniquely Spanish event from the very first time I set foot inside a bullring, the Monumental arena in Barcelona.

Dad had booked three tickets for us to go to the Monumental that afternoon, at five o'clock, that being the traditional time for many bullfights to start, as it is then that the heat of the Spanish sun starts to diminish. It is interesting that the tickets are sold as *sombre*, meaning in the shade, or *sol y sombre*, sun and shade. Imagine if tickets to football matches in this country were sold on that particular basis. I suppose it would be wet or dry.

We headed downstairs into the lobby at about four o'clock to get a taxi to the bullring and upon the lift doors opening, we saw a mêlée of photographers swarming around the lobby. It looked as if a film star had arrived at our hotel, until we managed to see exactly what all the fuss was about.

The three matadors who were fighting at the Monumental that very afternoon had been staying at our hotel and, already changed into their gloriously colourful fighting uniforms, were in the process of being whisked away to the bullring in a blacked-out limousine. I recognised one of them, as he was one of the most celebrated matadors fighting on the circuit. His name was Antonio Ordonez and it was more than likely his presence in the hotel which was causing all this commotion and press hysteria. Top matadors are treated as iconic figures in Spain and are usually given the all-star treatment one would normally associate with a pop star, or in the current celebrity-based climate, a top Premiership footballer.

The press attention subsided as our three matadors were driven away swiftly from the front entrance of the hotel, making their way to the bullring, next to be seen, by us anyway, coming face to face with half a ton of black fighting bull.

On our arrival at the Monumental, we made our way to our seats and I was fascinated to notice that tucked away, deep underneath the stands of the bullring, was a tiny chapel just large enough to accommodate one person. Dad, being totally fascinated by this discovery, asked one of the stewards in his best Spanish what it was there for and on receiving his answer realised that it was quite obvious why there was a chapel situated inside a bullring. Being a predominantly Catholic country, this chapel was for the exclusive use of the matadors to offer up prayers before they took their chances against the bulls in the ring.

As a quick aside to the goings-on at the Mon-umental, and having touched on the subject of Dad's 'best' Spanish, I have to give him credit and say that after many, many trips to Spain and Gibraltar, he became almost fluent in the language, and was more than able to get by in most situations. However he was totally unable to master the accent that went with his undoubted fluency in Spanish. Consequently, he sometimes had trouble in making someone understand his Spanish as it was always delivered in a very British accent. This failure to be the ultimate Spanish speaker became somewhat of a family joke and he had to suffer many a jibe, mainly by myself I have to confess, at his non-existent accent. He took it all in good spirit and ended up laughing at himself. He often turned to me and said that when I could speak as well as he did, and have the guts to do it, then I had a right to criticise but until then I should keep quiet. I did end up achieving an 'O' level in Spanish but I never mastered it as well as Dad.

It was still stiflingly hot even though we were in the *sombre* seats. The *corrida* was due to begin at any second and the atmosphere could be cut with the proverbial knife. A brass band played a traditional *paso doble* to welcome the entrance of the matadors and mark the official beginning of the afternoon's fighting.

You couldn't get anything more Spanish than an afternoon at the bullfight but what is strange is that nine times out of ten the members of the band which played the *paso doble* were English. It sounds odd, I agree, but having spoken to many bullfighting aficionados, I am assured it is a fact. Is it that the Spanish as a race have an inherent inability to blow a brass musical instrument?

What follows in terms of the actual bullfight will be left to your imagination, and I will not bore you with the literally gory details, but rest assured that the score ends up as Human Beings Six, Bulls Nil. This tends always to be the score, but on very rare occasions a matador does get fatally wounded. Serves him right is some people's retort to that, but I repeat, this is a topic of controversy which is still raging to this day and will never be resolved I fear.

The long-term effect of Dad going to the *corrida* on many occasions was that he started to realise that perhaps there was a market for a bullfighting game aimed directly at the passionate Spanish devotee. This was typical, of course, of Dad's mindset that he thought almost anything within reason could be turned into some form of game and his mind was constantly open for any small idea that came his way. A bullfighting game would be a difficult one, for he was never one really to go down the normal 'board game' route but instead tried always to 'Subbuteo-ise' any embryonic idea.

On a few occasions, he had seen me sitting at a restaurant table, bored with what was happening around me, and watched as I stuck wooden toothpicks into each corner of a bread roll and two picks to represent horns to make a crude model of a bull, and then proceeded to use two more picks as banderillas, the darts used in the bullfight, and sat there amused as I tried to kill this bread roll in the style of a matador. Perhaps this would be the route to go down: a really hands-on type of game. It then occurred to him that perhaps utilising the repulsion properties of two magnets could be a good way of recreating the almost balletic movement that occurs between a bull and a matador.

He even went as far as producing some very rudimentary prototypes, using these magnets with bull and fighter figures placed on top, to see how they would react and then assess if any form of game could be devised around this magnetic reaction. The magnetic repulsion seemed to work quite well initially, but Dad had trouble in visualising how this could be incorporated into a viable game, and most importantly, a game which would fit nicely into a niche that would be one hundred per cent recognisable as coming from the now famous stable of Subbuteo inventions. This was one idea that soon had a very quick demise, but it just shows how tuned in Dad's mind was to any possible new and original openings there might be in the games market. I suppose it was an inbred passion that was never to die.

Passion of a completely different nature was just around the corner at the flamenco club, Los Tarantos. Dad was spending more and more time at this particular club and those closest to him, mainly his Barcelona business associates, but most certainly not Mum or indeed me, as we were not accompanying him to Barcelona as frequently as we had been in the past, were getting a little concerned that perhaps he was getting into something which he was finding a great deal of difficulty getting out of.

The real truth was that most evenings Dad would make his way to the club in the early evening and sit at a table in front of the stage, drinking carafes of the house red wine and chain-smoking the most ghastly Spanish cigarettes. And he was there for one reason and one reason only and it was most definitely the flamenco dancing. In fact, it was a flamenco dancer who was a regular performer at the club. Over the previous few weeks and months Dad had struck up a very deep relationship with her. If something, or indeed someone in this particular case, grabbed his fancy he went all out to pursue the object of his desire, no matter what the ensuing consequences might be.

The dancer was named Rosario. Whether that was her stage or real name, I don't know for sure, but I never heard Dad mention a surname in connection with her. It was always the "lovely" Rosario. She was a lot younger than Dad, in her early twenties, this being the optimum age for any flamenco dancer at the top of her career. Dancers start their decline, career wise, in their late twenties and early thirties, a little like professional footballers. Dad was in his early fifties, so it was quite conceivable that he was old enough to be her father. Like any Spanish, or indeed Latin, woman she was in her prime at this age, and Dad obviously found her very attractive.

The obvious question which always tends to rear its head in these circumstances is what did a beautiful young woman in the prime of her life find remotely attractive or endearing about a man in his early fifties. Well, in Dad's case, and I have witnessed this first hand, he had an uncanny ability to turn on the charm at will, and any woman would be totally taken in by the compliments coated in thick syrup which oozed from his mouth. All this sounds extremely nauseating, I agree, but you had to be there to witness his technique, and to be honest, it wasn't really that sickly. It came over as quite natural, completely honest and genuine, as I believe he meant it to be.

I think, of course, he played the Subbuteo card as well, which he tended to use very sparingly indeed, and only when he thought it was an appropriate moment. Subbuteo was now a household name in Spain, and in Barcelona it was particularly well known because, like in Tunbridge Wells, the home workers were increasing in number by the day. Without doubt, Rosario would have been at least aware of the Subbuteo brand, and most probably thought it was quite a coup to be intimately involved with the founder and big chief of Subbuteo, even though he was a good many years her senior. To sum up, Dad could be a charmer and he would use this to marvellous effect at will, even in his business dealings if the situation warranted it.

There were to be many cloak and dagger meetings between Dad and Rosario and he would often jet off with her to various European destinations for maybe a weekend or perhaps even a week at a time, depending on her own work and indeed Dad's work commitments at the time. As far as Mum and I were concerned, he was just away on business in either Spain or Gibraltar. He covered his tracks very well where Rosario was concerned and his planning was at times not dissimilar to a military operation. His downfall in the Rosario affair, however, was trusting in a third party to cover his tracks.

Rosario was due to undertake a small UK tour with her flamenco troupe, taking in small clubs around the country, to give us British a taster of what real flamenco was all about. One of the venues was to be a three-night stint at a Spanish club-cum-restaurant in the heart of London's Soho and so Dad had arranged accommodation for himself and Rosario at a hotel not far from the venue. It was not one of the nicest hotels, not the type of place in which Dad was used to staying, but it was only for a few nights and it was convenient for Rosario as far as her work was concerned.

As always, he told Mum that he would be going to Barcelona for a few days to, as he explained to us, oversee the opening of some new Subbuteo premises. To make this ruse seem more plausible and authentic, he enlisted the help of a close friend and business colleague, who shall remain nameless in order to protect the innocent becoming guilty by association, and who just happened genuinely to be going to Barcelona on Subbuteo business on the same few days that Rosario and Dad were shacked up together in their London hideaway.

The idea was that Dad was to give his colleague a pre-written postcard of Barcelona, addressed to Mum and myself at home in Langton Green, with the strictest of instructions that on his arrival in Barcelona he was to purchase a stamp, stick it on the postcard and post it, hence giving Mum and me the impression that Dad was in Barcelona on business as we assumed he was. Why would anyone think any different on receipt of a postcard with 'Greetings from Barcelona' emblazoned on the front, together with a Spanish stamp and postmark on it?

The colleague was duly despatched to the airport to catch his flight to Barcelona, with the postcard secured about his person. With everything going on at the airport, the palaver of checking in and going through customs, he must have had some kind of mental block with regard to his exact instructions concerning the despatch of the card. Panicking, and thinking that he had forgotten to do as he had been asked, he swiftly bought a stamp – an English stamp – stuck it on the postcard and posted it in a letterbox – an English letterbox – at the airport and swiftly continued on his way through customs, happy and relieved that he had carried out Dad's instructions to the letter.

Mum received the famous postcard a few days later and I don't think she spotted right away that it was a communication from Spain, bearing an English stamp and English postmark. It was only when she read the card again a few hours later that she spotted this incriminating error.

She had no idea where on earth Dad was for he most certainly was not in Spain, so it was just a question of playing a waiting game and seeing what he had to say for himself when he eventually came breezing back into the family home, saying what a worthwhile but very tiring and hectic business trip he had just had in Barcelona.

Four or five days later Dad did come breezing back home, but he had no time at all to mention any fictitious trip to Spain before Mum had angrily thrust the evidence right under his nose and asked him to explain himself.

What could he say really? Nothing at all. The evidence of his infidelity was there in front him as plain as day. It was no use making up some pathetic excuse, as that would be digging an even bigger hole than the one he was already in. He decided to own up to his liaison with the flamenco dancer from Barcelona and suffer the flack which was surely heading his way.

Mum was quite rightly extremely upset and felt totally betrayed by Dad's actions and, after a great deal of pleading from him, decided that she was not going to throw him out, on the understanding that he never, ever pulled this type of stunt again. I think under the circumstances she was being very lenient.

But future trips to Spain and Gibraltar, either for business or pleasure, were monitored very closely by Mum, and if possible Dad had to delegate any such trips to other senior members of the Subbuteo staff. He had had his wings well and truly clipped this time.

Chapter 8

Celebrity Encounters

THE DICTIONARY DEFINITION of the word celebrity is *the condition of being much talked about; famousness; notoriety.* Today, almost anyone can become a celebrity. You need only look at the so-called reality television shows to see that. Unknowns plucked from obscurity and thrust in front of the cameras for the delectation of the general public. These people are not talented by any stretch of the imagination, but somehow they seem to worm their way into our consciousness through the power of that big metal box which sits in the corner of most living rooms. It is only when you stand back and see them for what they really are that you wonder why on earth we tolerate and hold these people in such high esteem. You or I could do what they are doing and be earning big bucks from it to boot. Celebrity wanted: no talent required, seems to be the order of the day.

Before the onset of these hideous shows, and the newfangled technology that enables us to have hundreds of television channels at our disposal, in the days when we were limited to just three channels, the word celebrity was a just and reasonable description of anyone in the public eye. They earned their stripes and in turn merited the respect of the general public. In whichever field of entertainment they were in, be it acting, singing, playing football or cricket, these people had talent. It was all wheat and no chaff.

It was through Subbuteo that Dad had the good fortune to meet a few of these celebrities of the fifties, sixties and seventies. Some of the encounters were by pure chance because he frequented the same establishments they did, or they were engineered encounters, not because he had any great desire to meet whoever it was, but because it was necessary to further his business plans and ideas. Most of them, however, fell into the former category.

There are a few which have a decidedly tenuous link to this particular chapter, but I might as well include them anyway. For a start, David Niven, the famous actor, lived at the bottom of our garden. I know that makes it sound like he was a part-time gnome or a little woodland creature, but that was the family term for explaining to anyone the remotest bit interested who our immediate neighbours were. I use the word 'lived' in the loosest possible way, for he had a house there, but most of the time he was away working, doing whatever David Niven did to enable him to afford a house at the end of our garden. I'm not sure if anyone in the village had ever spoken to him, but I'm pretty sure Mum and Dad hadn't.

There was a very popular police detective series on television during the sixties called 'Jason King', with the starring role being taken by an actor named Peter Wyngarde. His trademark was the big hair and droopy moustache which was a popular look, and he wore loud shirts and matching ties. He lived in Langton Green and could often be seen cruising around the village, looking exactly as he did on television, in his bright green Lotus Europa sports car. A very flamboyant character indeed. He stuck out like the proverbial sore thumb in the rather conservative surroundings of our village. It had always been my ambition as a youngster to own a Lotus Europa, probably from seeing his example around and about. Mr Wyngarde was aware that Subbuteo was produced in his home village because Dad said he made enquiries at the factory about getting hold of a game for himself. But Dad never met him as he was away on business at the time he called. He was told that the factory was unable to supply him with his game and that he should obtain one through the usual retail outlets. I think he was just after a celebrity freebie. Perhaps he approached Lotus in the same manner.

One of Dad's many watering holes in the Tunbridge Wells area was a pub in the centre of the town, The Bedford Arms. It was opposite the railway station and many of its clientele were commuters who popped in for a swift one after getting off the train from London in the evening. Whenever Dad went in there he struck up a conversation with a scruffy-looking gentleman, with a rather hangdog expression, who permanently sat up at the bar nursing the same pint of beer all evening.

He was one of those characters who seemingly did not have a good word to say about anyone or anything and appeared to be in a permanent state of grumpiness. Even if he was bought a drink, not a smile crossed his face and he accepted it with barely a word of thanks. Even so, for some reason Dad got on strangely well with him, and despite his rather grumpy demeanour and offhand manner, he was indeed a gentleman in the most literal sense of the word. That's probably why Dad took to him. On one occasion, Dad went to the bar to order his usual lunchtime pint and offered to buy one for our friend as well.

The barman mentioned in passing that it must be Bob's lucky day as everyone seemed to want to buy him a drink that day. So that was his name – Bob. It never occurred to Dad to ask the old boy's name. It was Bob Todd, the comedy actor. Who? I hear you ask. Remember 'the Benny Hill Show' in the early seventies? Bob Todd was Benny Hill's sidekick in the show, his straight man. You must remember him. No? Oh well, he was fairly well known at the time – if you liked Benny Hill.

A year that Dad would remember for a very long time was 1964. A particular genre of music was making its mark on Britain, if not the world. This was being called the Merseybeat by journalists in the know because a lot of the new bands came from the Liverpool area. There were bands like Gerry and the Pacemakers, the Searchers, the Swinging Blue Jeans, to name but a few and then, of course, the most famous band who hailed from Liverpool, the Beatles. Beatlemania was rife at the time and everywhere you went there was Beatles' merchandise for sale, from mugs, tea towels, wall clocks, even underwear, but the one thing that was not available, strangely enough, were models of the group themselves.

Dad picked up on this gap in the market and immediately saw a way to cash in himself on the popularity of the Beatles and make a quick buck. He had all the right contacts, and indeed know-how, to set the ball rolling, but the one thing he lacked was permission from the group themselves or at least their management. Having been bitten by the Stanley Matthews incident some fifteen years earlier he was not prepared to go down that road again so he decided to go through the correct procedures and channels.

The first thing though was to get an idea of what these figures would look like before embarking on the copyright aspect and take it from there. He approached a renowned model-maker named Charles Stadden, whom Subbuteo and Dad had used on previous occasions. He was an expert in his field, producing, among other works of art, military figures in the finest detail for the toy firm Britains. Helped by numerous photos of the group, Stadden produced four beautifully crafted, hand-painted two-and-a-half inch high figures of John, Paul, George and Ringo in lead. The facial resemblance was uncanny, considering how small their faces were. I am lucky enough to own these actual lead figures and they are a one-off, but unfortunately, Paul has mislaid his bass guitar over the years which spoils it somewhat – my claim is that Paul McCartney was the first 'air guitarist'. I had these figures valued quite recently by a Beatles Memorabilia site on the internet and I was told that at auction they could fetch anything between £10-£15,000.

Having seen and approved the lead castings Dad felt it was worth a shot at marketing them. Nothing ventured nothing gained, as the old adage goes, which was really Dad's way of working. He now had to set about the rather difficult task of getting the approval of the parties concerned. So he wrote to the Beatles' management company outlining in great detail his plans for the figures and asked if it was possible to set up a meeting to discuss the copyright aspect of his proposed plan. To his utter amazement he received a reply back almost immediately saying that Brian Epstein, the Beatles' manager, was away in America for the foreseeable future but would welcome a meeting with Dad in New York if he could make it over there. Well, Dad could not believe his luck, and at once started to get the ball rolling, organising flights, hotels in New York, that sort of thing.

So in the autumn of 1964 Dad found himself sitting in the foyer of the Plaza Hotel, New York City, awaiting his much anticipated and important meeting with Brian Epstein. He was duly summoned to a suite of rooms on one of the top floors of the hotel and there he was greeted by Mr Epstein, but he was not alone – Paul and Ringo were in residence as well. Dad was quite taken aback, as you might imagine, as nothing had been mentioned about any Beatle being there. Dad thought it was to be a one-to-one meeting with the manager. After many hours of negotiation Dad emerged from the hotel suite having signed an agreement with Brian Epstein to manufacture and distribute the figures worldwide,

His mission was now complete. He returned home to Langton Green with much enthusiasm about his trip and how he met half of the Beatles. I clearly remember him holding his right hand out to me and telling me that this was the hand which shook the hand of Paul McCartney and that he would never wash it again as long as he lived.

The figures sold reasonably well throughout America and Great Britain, and there were plans afoot to produce other pop stars of the day. Charles Stadden produced samples of Gerry and the Pacemakers, Cilla Black, the Dave Clark Five and Freddie and the Dreamers, but these were never produced for the retail market.

Now the Beatles figures are highly collectable, not only among Subbuteo collectors (no mention of Subbuteo was made on the packaging), and a mint set in its original packaging can fetch around £1,000 I read very recently that Paul McCartney was keen to get hold of a set of these figures and tried in vain to contact him via his management company to see if he was interested in my unique lead castings. Not that I am all that eager to sell them you understand, but if Paul McCartney was to offer me silly money I would have to seriously consider the situation.

It could be said that there is an emerging theme here: that a few of these encounters took place in either upmarket hotels or drinking establishments. That's fair enough as Dad did spend a good number of his waking hours frequenting these places and it was in these surroundings that he felt most at ease. The following is no exception.

I am not quite sure how Dad ended up in Hong Kong in 1978, but the fact of the matter is that he did and he found it to be one of the most fascinating places he had ever visited. As always, he did not scrimp on his choice of accommodation, and had booked himself into the best hotel, the five-star Mandarin Oriental. The services on offer went way beyond anything that one might expect from a similar hotel in Europe.

On his first evening he was making an enquiry at the hotel reception about local restaurants, and the best places at which to sample the nightlife, when the receptionist produced a leather-bound directory of hostesses available as companions for the evening. All Dad had to do was choose one, and after a quick phone call from the hotel his chosen lady would meet him in the foyer in about twenty minutes or at an agreed time. The bottom line was that they were high-class prostitutes, but masquerading under the title of hostesses or companions. Wrap it up how you like, but it boils down to the same end product.

Dad was amazed at how open and above board the staff at the hotel were about offering this type of service, as if they were showing him a wine list or menu or something like that. He did actually look through the directory, more as a point of interest than anything else (yeah, right!), but he did admit to me that for a split second he was very tempted to choose a hostess that caught his eye, to accompany him on his first evening out, but thought better of it as firstly Mum was at home and secondly it would have cost him many, many Hong Kong dollars.

Venturing into one of the hotel's many bars, he settled down in a corner, ordered a drink and contemplated where he should spend his first evening in this marvellously vibrant city. The bar was now filling up with hotel guests and non-residents, mainly Hong Kong business people taking in a drink in the relaxing atmosphere after a long day at work.

A woman appeared and sat at the table next to him, and Dad could not help but notice how attractive she was and how her almost Indian appearance made her stand out from the rest of the people in the bar. He nodded to her in acknowledgement of her presence, continued with his drink and she was soon joined by her companion, presumably her husband, a tall man in his mid-forties, with blond hair and wearing the most obvious pair of thick-rimmed glasses. Dad thought that if you're going to wear glasses, at least make them blend in with your face a little. That was typical of him; he tended to be quite opinionated at times and if he hadn't been on his own would probably have made some comment on this man's glasses, usually in a loud voice so that the target of his comments would probably have heard and Dad would have to be told to keep his voice down.

Another extremely annoying habit, and at times a very embarrassing one, was his penchant for listening to other people's conversations, a trait he definitely inherited from his mother. With this couple sitting so close to him Dad could not help but try as best he could to eavesdrop on their conversation, and it soon became clear that the gentleman in the glasses was definitely English, but with a very pronounced

London accent, which fascinated Dad as the accent did not entirely match his looks.

Curiosity got the better of him at last and Dad leaned over, excused himself for interrupting and asked if they were English, which was somewhat of a rhetorical question, as he knew all too well that at least the man was. The reply came back in the affirmative and Dad was asked if he was on his own, and if so, would he like to join them for a drink.

Dad left his seat and crossed over to join the couple, introducing himself, and in turn the couple introduced themselves as Michael and Shakira. You might have guessed by now who Dad was drinking with but he had no idea at all.

To him they were just English people abroad who had met up and were passing the time of day. Michael invited Dad to join him and his wife for dinner in the hotel, so that at least would solve the dilemma as to where he would be eating that night, and Dad accepted on the proviso that he would not be encroaching and that he would pay his own way, which went without saying.

The dinner menu offered a wide range of food from across the world with the emphasis being on Chinese cuisine quite naturally. And while his hosts tucked into some of the local delicacies, Dad, being extremely conservative in his taste for food, opted for a steak, which he could have eaten anywhere. He had this revulsion for garlic and onions and would go to extreme lengths to make sure that any meal he was eating contained absolutely no traces of these. If it did, it would be sent back to the kitchen.

Throughout the meal Dad noticed that the waiters seemed to be paying a great deal of attention to his table, perhaps more than any other, and he wondered why this should be. Other diners would at times glance over to where the three of them were seated, stare for a while and then continue eating their meal. Most strange.

Dad was asked by Michael what he did for a living and in his usual way, said that he was the ex-proprietor of Subbuteo and had Michael heard of it. Dad was chuffed to learn that Michael had indeed heard of his baby and that, although not a prolific player, used to play when he was younger, when filming commitments allowed.

Filming commitments? Intrigued by this, Dad asked what filming commitments and Michael, surprised that Dad had not already guessed who he was, asked if he had heard of or seen the film *The Italian Job*, and also the Harry Palmer series. Dad said of course he knew those films and suddenly the penny dropped. He had spent all evening drinking and eating with Michael Caine and his beautiful wife Shakira and he had only just realised. He felt extremely stupid for not having clicked earlier and then he realised why the extra attention had been shown to them by staff and clientele alike. Dad apologised profusely and they both told him not to be so stupid and that it didn't matter. In fact, Michael said that it made a pleasant change for him not to be recognised and that he was able to enjoy his meal without being asked the same old repetitive questions and to sign autographs.

The evening came to an end and Dad made his way back to the bar for a nightcap before retiring to his room. Michael and Shakira were invited to join him for a last drink but as they were leaving Hong Kong the next day they declined and made their way to their room, thanking Dad for his company and a very pleasant evening.

The next day Dad phoned Mum back in England and told her to guess with whom he had had dinner the previous night. When he told her it was Michael Caine, she did not believe him at first, but after a little persuasion from Dad that it was all true, she felt a tiny bit miffed that she had missed out as she had always had a soft spot for Michael Caine. Not a lot of people knew that!

Finally in this chapter, I would like to indulge myself and tell of my own Subbuteo-related celebrity encounter. I am sure that if Dad had been with us he would have been asked to take part and it probably would have taken on more significance. But he wasn't therefore I was next in the pecking order so to speak. In March 2004, I was contacted out of the blue by a researcher from a television production company called Flame Productions and was informed that they were in the process of getting together a documentary programme for ITV to be hosted by Chris Tarrant and his wife Ingrid and it was to be called 'Tarrant's Way'. The main premise of the show was that Chris and Ingrid were to follow the first ever illustrated AA road map, originally published in the 1950s, from their home in London, driving Ingrid's father's 1938 Derby Bentley convertible.

They hoped to discover how life had altered from the time the original map was published and explore the history and interesting facts about the towns they visited on their way. They were to visit Tunbridge Wells and were keen to know if I would like to be filmed and interviewed about the Subbuteo story.

Of course, I jumped at this opportunity and agreed at once to do it. I came off the phone rather excited but after a while, when I had calmed down, realised what I had let myself in for. It would be rather nerve-racking but I assured myself that it would be enormous fun and that it was something Dad would have wanted me to do and he would have been proud of me. The date for filming had been arranged for 23rd July and I was to meet the film and production crew at the original Subbuteo factory in Langton Green at three o'clock.

I was just on the verge of leaving home to go to the old factory with my son Tom, who wanted to meet Chris Tarrant and also take some photos and watch the filming, when I received a phone call from the production assistant to say that the Bentley had broken down about twenty minutes away and that it should soon be up and running again after some emergency adjustments and could we meet at five o'clock instead? I had been gearing myself up all day for three o'clock and now I had to wait for a further couple of hours. Still, that's old cars for you.

It had been a typically English summer's day – drizzling with rain. So by the time everyone had arrived at the factory for filming they were well and truly hacked off. The plan was to film Chris and Ingrid arriving at the factory, but in true movie tradition the beginning was filmed at the end when the rain had stopped and the evening sunshine had decided to appear in all its glory.

I knew Chris had arrived because I saw the Bentley parked up, so set off to find him and the crew in the old factory. I introduced myself and found him a lovely man. He was very relaxed, and immediately started talking to me about Subbuteo and Dad, but almost as soon as he had started he stopped and said that it was best if he didn't know too much before filming started as it would come across more naturally if he was to ask anything he needed to know on camera. It seemed logical to me.

I had taken my original Subbuteo pitch and a couple of teams with me to the shoot, one of which was QPR quite naturally, and we were all set up and ready to go when Ingrid appeared. What a lovely women she was. She seemed genuinely interested in the whole Subbuteo story, and as well as her and Chris interviewing me on camera, she took the time off camera to talk to me about Subbuteo and Dad with the utmost fascination. The actual filming was a very relaxed procedure and to be honest I didn't realise the cameras were rolling as there seemed to be a seamless transition between off camera chat and the actual recording which I suppose is done on purpose to put the interviewee at ease. Very clever and I needed that.

Between various takes, Tom and I spent the time in general chit-chat with Chris, not particularly about Subbuteo, and it seemed very surreal talking to someone whom you had seen on the television a lot, about exceedingly mundane topics. Everything was soon 'in the can', to use the correct parlance, and I packed my Subbuteo table and teams away in the car. But there was just one more thing I had to do before I left. Being prepared, I had brought along with me a copy of the *Who wants to be a Millionaire?* quiz book and asked Chris to sign it. How sad is that?

He duly obliged and also posed for some photos with Tom which I took. We said our goodbyes to Chris, Ingrid and the crew and went home looking forward to seeing the episode on television in late November. I have to admit to being slightly disappointed as I was under the impression that it was to be shown on the entire ITV region, but was in fact broadcast on ITV London only. Never mind, I did make it onto the telly. Andy Warhol, the renowned 1960s artist and icon of the psychedelic era, once stated that, "In the future everyone will be world-famous for fifteen minutes." I'm not so sure about the world part, but he was correct about the time duration. How *did* he know?!

Chapter 9

Selling and the post-Subbuteo Years

IF YOU WERE to ask any person who had been employed by Subbuteo, they would always say that Dad had the ability to know his employees personally and he knew what their role was in the company from the part-time worker right up to the highest managerial position. They were, of course, human beings, not just a number on a payroll and a cog in the machine. He knew if they were happy or if there was an underlying problem preventing them from fulfilling their role to its maximum potential.

He took the time, even with a heavy work schedule, to walk around the factory floor and pass the time of day with each individual and that, I feel, eliminated the divide which quite often occurs between management and staff: the us and them scenario. Their reaction to this was a mutual respect and the staff referred to him affectionately as Mr P or PA or the more formal Mr Adolph, but never, ever was he called Peter.

They knew that they should never cross that fine line, and if they did, I am sure that Dad would have politely pointed out the error of their ways and the relationship would have been placed back on an even keel. If any employee overstepped the mark in a major way, he would have been down on them like a ton of bricks and if necessary relieved them of their position or, to put it in a more common manner, he would have given them the boot. He was firm but fair and everyone seemed to like him as an employer.

I remember quite clearly one particular evening he was in a foul mood for some reason and both Mum and I thought he had just had one of those bad days, which we all have from time to time. Literally a bad day at the office. Perhaps he had had an argument with someone or a supplier had let him down and was unable to meet a deadline, that sort of thing. After a great deal of digging and trying to find out exactly what his problem was, it transpired that a member of staff had knocked on his door during the afternoon, sat down in front of Dad and had asked for a pay rise. How dare they ask for more money!

This kind of request used to send Dad's blood pressure sky high and he always got this simple request out of all proportion. Apparently, the employee was a highly regarded member of staff and was well within his rights to ask for an increase in his wages. He was by no means a passenger on the good ship Subbuteo, but Dad fobbed him off with an excuse for not granting his wishes and said he would get back to him at a later date when he had the time and inclination to review the situation. He then proceeded to take out his frustrations on his nearest and dearest. Thanks a lot.

Dad's banishment from the family home for his indiscretions was taking its toll on his ability to put his mind fully to the job in hand at Subbuteo and, armed with this useful excuse, he managed to persuade Mum that for the sake of the business and my own well-being he should be allowed to return to his rightful place across the road at Little Pryors. At first, Mum was reluctant to agree as she was always one to stick rigidly to any decisions she might have made, particularly one as important as this. She managed to see Dad's point of view eventually, and mainly for my sake agreed to take him back home on a trial basis.

It was not long after his return that Dad, for the first time ever in the history of Subbuteo, realised that his total and overall command of what was happening in his beloved business was starting to wane. He was on the telephone one afternoon, gazing out of his office window across the garden at Upper Birchetts, when he saw an unfamiliar figure going up and down the iron staircase which led up to the store. This person was carrying large cardboard boxes to a delivery van which was waiting to despatch games to the retail outlets.

Dad had never met or spoken to this person before and started to make enquiries around the office and factory to find out the identity of this complete stranger. It turned out that he was a new employee who had been engaged a few days earlier to help in the despatch department and his employment had been sanctioned by the personnel office which was located in a converted bedroom on the top floor. Perhaps personnel office is a little too flowery a description as it was really the woman who also did the payroll but who had been given responsibility to authorise the engagement of all factory staff.

This authority had been given to her by Dad only a few weeks previously, but it still hit home to him quite suddenly that he was no longer able to do everything and that mundane tasks like recruiting factory staff had to be done by someone else. After many years of having his finger on the pulse of every single aspect of the business, he realised that it was far bigger than he had ever imagined and that he was coming to a crossroads in the development and progress of Subbuteo. On one hand, he wanted the business to grow and grow but also, on the other hand, he wanted it to remain as much like a cottage industry as was possible. He soon accepted that he could not have both.

I am a great believer that situations have a tendency to sort themselves out without any intervention from any individual. Perhaps I could be called a fatalist or just maybe coincidences are to blame, but not long after the aforementioned episode with the unrecognised employee and the sudden realisation that went with it, Dad was contacted out of the blue by giant toy manufacturers John Waddington of Leeds, whose most famous products were, and indeed still are, the Monopoly and Cluedo board games.

They were inquiring whether Dad was interested in selling Subbuteo to them as they had seen and heard of the massive impact the game was having on the current retail market, and not surprisingly they wanted a piece, if not the whole, of the action. This approach caused Dad a great deal of anxiety as he really did not know what the correct course of action should be.

He mulled it over and spent many hours burning the midnight oil with Mum, discussing the pros and cons of this scenario that had suddenly manifested itself. He felt that a compromise would be to sell a percentage of his business so that he would still have a controlling interest in what was after all his very own conception. The thought of handing the whole operation over lock, stock and barrel would be too much for him to consider, and with this in mind he wrote to Waddingtons, thanking them for their interest in Subbuteo, and stating that he would only really be interested in their offer if they were prepared to take a thirty-five per cent stake.

Within days Dad received a communication back from Waddingtons stating that they were not interested in a part stake in Subbuteo, that for any deal to go ahead they would require a one hundred per cent stake in the company. All or nothing. This reply again set Dad, and indeed Mum, thinking about the long-term implications of the offer. They decided all parties concerned should meet face to face and discuss the finer points of any possible deal. It was arranged for Dad to meet Waddingtons chairman, Victor Watson, and his board of directors at their headquarters in Leeds.

This was to be proceeded by a delegation from Waddingtons coming to Tunbridge Wells to cast their eyes over the whole Subbuteo operation and to get a feel as to how the business was run and if any improvements could be made in the event of any possible takeover.

The powers that be at Waddingtons were quite

impressed with what they saw happening at Subbuteo, but quite naturally they picked up on a few points in the operation that needed to be improved, which if Subbuteo became part of a larger conglomerate, would be quite easily implemented.

As Mum was a named director of Subbuteo and all its subsidiaries, it quite naturally followed that she would accompany Dad to Leeds for all the possible takeover negotiations. But this caused a little confrontation. On arrival at Waddington headquarters in Leeds, the chairman, indeed the entire board, made it quite clear that they did not wish Mum to be present at the negotiations. Reading between the lines it was obvious that this was because she was a woman, and women should have no input into such delicate negotiations.

Of course, this attitude made Dad see red before they had even sat down around the negotiating table and he made it abundantly clear that his wife was a bona fide director of Subbuteo in her own right and that any talks would include her. If not, the whole thing would be called off and they would depart back to Tunbridge Wells. I think that Waddingtons got the idea, and quite rightly Mum was included in the forthcoming negotiations. Her input was eventually highly regarded. It was rather a stormy beginning to the talks which did not ease any tension, but very soon the atmosphere quickly developed into one of mutual respect. As the hours went by it soon became apparent that Waddingtons were sticking hard and fast to their demand for a one hundred per cent controlling stake in Subbuteo.

With a few compromises Dad soon agreed that he would be more than happy to sell Subbuteo on this basis. An initial figure of around £230,000 was agreed upon, with an upfront, goodwill cash payment of £150,000. The balance would be paid in Waddington 'B' shares. These things take time to finalise and when it was all done and dusted the final figure was a far more realistic £250,000. Subbuteo was now a wholly owned subsidiary of John Waddington.

One of the clauses in the final deal was that Dad would be kept on as a director of Subbuteo and consultant, mainly to ease the company through the early stages of its transitional period as a subsidiary of Waddingtons. The Waddington hierarchy soon realised very quickly the kind of man they had been dealing with in Dad over the preceding negotiation period. They knew that he had a mind that was always tuned in to any possible new openings in the toys and games market, and they were quite right. Just because he had sold his brainchild, which had made him quite a wealthy man, it did not mean that he would instantly stop thinking of new ideas. Because of this a clause in his consultancy contract stated that he was not to develop any game which infringed upon any product currently produced by Waddingtons and that now included Subbuteo.

Dad's consultancy period with Waddingtons was an extremely rocky affair because he found it very difficult to be just a cog in a machine, not being able to have the ultimate say in any decision. He was just not cut out to be a company 'suit'. He disagreed very strongly indeed over many decisions Waddingtons made over the Subbuteo transition despite being a consultant. They seemed to know better than he did when it came to Subbuteo and it really did seem pointless that he had been made a consultant in the first place.

He might as well not have bothered and as time went on it became crystal clear to Dad that the consultancy post was intended to be a lever in the initial sales negotiations and that Waddingtons had very little intention of taking on board Dad's input as far as Subbuteo was concerned. It soon became too much to bear and he had an enormous showdown with the board of directors, informing them exactly what he thought of them and in no uncertain terms telling them what they could do with their consultancy position.

Despite the board trying to placate him and saying that they would try to be more open to any input from Dad in the future, he thought deep down that any promises and reassurances which came from the mouths of the board were just a load of hot air. He decided enough was enough and stood down from his consultancy post. Something inside him would not let the matter drop and he left with this strong feeling that he had to get even with them in some way; that, despite his undying love for Subbuteo, the best way to retaliate would be to go against any previous clause in a now worthless contract and see if he could bring out a game in direct conflict to Subbuteo. Even if nothing came of it, Dad would feel that he would in a strange way be having the parting shot and that he was not to be messed with.

Bringing out a rival game would not be difficult as he still had many contacts in the business and they were loyal contacts who would be more than willing to help him out in this project. Although he did not really care whether he would be infringing any copyright or contract clause, Dad realised that to cover himself he needed to find a loophole somewhere which would exonerate him personally in the event of the situation becoming out of control and the finger being pointed directly at him for any breach of conduct. The most obvious loophole in all this was that Mum had the same initials as him, P A Adolph, and there were certainly no restraints on her so any future product would be marketed simply under the initials P A Adolph and M P Adolph, which is myself. Mum and I would be registered as sole directors of any future company. Simple and straightforward and completely watertight. No comeback whatsoever on Dad. He would enjoy taunting Waddingtons over this one if ever push came to shove.

So what would this new product be? The most obvious would be a complete copy of Subbuteo but a much better and updated version with a few added accessories thrown in for good measure. This was to be a product born out of anger and resentment and if one was to go deep inside the mind of Dad, it was obvious it did not matter to him one iota if it was a success or a complete failure, which to be honest it was destined to be. The motivation was to have the final say over the dinosaur which was John Waddington and prove to himself that this was not the end of Peter Adolph, games inventor and the driving force behind Subbuteo.

I was fourteen years old and when Dad approached me to have some input into this new and clearly very devious venture, I thought it was the greatest honour ever to have been bestowed upon someone so young. Although he was my Dad first and foremost, he was also Mr Subbuteo and to be consulted on such a project was fantastic. I had been asked my opinion in the past over a few Subbuteo ideas that Dad had floating around his head but this was an opportunity to be involved from an embryonic stage.

I now knew how Dad felt when he was faced with the challenge to bring something fresh and innovative to the toys and games market, but alas this new concept was to be neither fresh nor indeed innovative, just a repackaged version of Subbuteo.

It did not take long for Dad to make contact with various manufacturers and within a relatively short space of time he had the moulds made for the figures and the bases; in fact, everything was in place to start moulding his game. The figures were slightly different from those in Subbuteo in that they were more in keeping with the then current football kits and, of course, they all had up-to-date hairstyles, which Subbuteo tended to ignore. A small detail maybe, but you would be surprised at how the general public can pick up on these minor details.

In his urgency to get the ball rolling on this new project, it suddenly occurred to Dad that he had not thought of a name for the game, so going along the same route that had served him so well over the past years, he decided to call the game Aquila, the Latin name for eagle. It had also been used as a company name for a subsidiary of Subbuteo in Spain.

He engaged the services of a renowned artist by the name of Gary Keane to do the artwork for the box, someone he had used many years before for certain Subbuteo editions. Gary Keane at the time was working for the *Daily Express*, drawing a regular feature in the newspaper for tips and ideas for improving your golfing technique, using drawings of the golfer Gary Player. His work did not come cheap but the resulting artwork was a pleasure to behold.

Something new was needed for the Aquila game that was not already available through Subbuteo and I came up with an idea which I initially called 'The Striker Figure', and this was what it ended up being called officially as there was really no better description for this piece of kit. It was a two-inch high footballer figure mounted on a spring which in turn was attached to a very heavy flat lead base for stability.

The idea was for this figure to be used during the game at set pieces, free kicks, corners, and the ball would hit the sprung figure and hopefully be directed towards the goal and sometimes even score. The figures were manufactured in a choice of three different poses for a bit of reality and this also had the added benefit of giving the ball a rather haphazard rebounding effect when it hit the figure. It was a simple idea which, of course, all the best ones are, and one that seemed to work very well. The way the ball rebounded into the net if it was hit correctly was a joy and you could almost imagine this action happening on a real football pitch.

Again the moulds were made for these Striker Figures, and thousands of them were produced in all the aforementioned various poses. Dad gave me the task of hand-painting them in as many different football strips as I could manage. This was a very enjoyable experience and one I found deeply engrossing. I whiled away many an hour during various school holidays and half-term breaks painting these figures and eventually I became quite proficient at it, although painting two-inch high figures is one thing; painting the actual 00 scale playing figures is quite another. The Striker Figure was to be included in the game set and it was not really intended to be an add-on accessory. But this idea was very soon to change. Prototype games were assembled and it was time for Waddingtons to be approached with the whole concept. Dad made it abundantly clear to them from the outset that this was nothing whatsoever to do with him. It was all the idea of Mum and my good self. I suppose from the Waddington point of view he was acting as our manager.

I am sure Waddingtons knew deep down that Dad was behind this, but they could never really prove anything. Not surprisingly, they took one look at the game and dismissed it immediately as nothing more than a plagiarised version of Subbuteo, which of course it was. However, they reluctantly showed a little bit of interest in my Striker Figure and Dad thought they might have been interested in making this a Subbuteo accessory.

Quickly latching on to their possible interest, Dad decided to do the hard sell on them, on our behalf of course, that this would complement the Subbuteo range of accessories, something that we had never intended the figure to do. This turned out to be a futile attempt as Waddingtons eventually turned down the Striker Figure, albeit after a great deal of consid-eration. I do believe had it been presented to them by someone other than an Adolph, they might have taken the plunge and added it to their range of accessories.

An enormous amount of money had been spent getting this game to the prototype stage and all for nothing really, although Dad felt it was money well spent just to have a final dig at Waddingtons. Their rejection of the Aquila game probably had an effect in the long term as only twelve of these games were ever produced and if any collector wanted to add one to his collection, it would set them back a fair few pounds, probably in the region of three hundred. Offers anyone?

By the mid-1970s things on the home front between Mum and Dad had not worked out as hoped. Dad's return to the family home from living above the factory was a short-term arrangement to see if they could still live together. The answer was a definite no, and although I believe there was still a certain amount of fondness between them, they seemed to spark off each other and family life was not as it should have been.

I was now eighteen years old and had left Eastbourne College and was going to a local college of further education to retake some 'O' levels which I had failed at school. My age and situation was a factor in what was now to happen as I was more independent than I obviously had been before, having just passed my driving test. And so Little Pryors was put up for sale and when it was sold Mum and Dad were to go their separate ways. The idea was for them each to buy a flat in Tunbridge Wells and I was then faced with one of the first major decisions of my young life. The three of us got together and I was told what the situation was between Mum and Dad, although I could see with my own eyes what was going on and I knew roughly what our family gathering was all about. What I did not anticipate, although I should have realised that it would eventually happen, was that I had to choose with whom I would be living when they eventually went their separate ways. How do you choose something like that?

Had I been younger, the decision would have been made for me, but now I was put in the position of having to choose. I made no immediate decision and I was reassured by both Mum and Dad that whatever I decided there would be no hard feelings and that my decision would be fully understood. After a good deal of thought and, despite their reassurances of complete understanding, an enormous amount of guilt on my shoulders, I made the agonising decision that I would move with Mum into her next home.

I have to confess that the decision was made purely on the basis that Mum could cater for my everyday needs, like cooking, doing the washing and a general feminine ability to run a successful home. Dad struggled to look after himself as far as cooking and general domestic chores were concerned so having me around as an untidy teenager would have been too much for him to cope with. I think he accepted my decision with great relief.

Little Pryors and the accompanying six acres of land were eventually sold for the princely sum of £35,000 which was at the top end of the housing market in the mid-seventies.

To put that into perspective, a two-up two-down semi-detached property in the South East of England at that time would have sold for somewhere in the region of £3,000. A similar property to Little Pryors nowadays would probably fetch around £1m. How times do change.

Mum and Dad managed to find suitable flats in Tunbridge Wells living only about a mile apart. That was far enough for them eventually to be able to be the best of friends and even go out on occasions for a meal or even a few drinks at the local pub. It was really a case of could not live with but could not live apart. Sometimes Dad would visit Mum in the evening for a meal and chat, and for some reason things would start to flare up between them and there would be an almighty argument and Mum would promptly kick Dad out of her flat and they would not speak again for a few weeks. It would always, without fail, be Dad who would offer up the olive branch and they would be friends again. A quite extraordinary relationship really.

One evening, on returning a little later than normal from college, I found Dad at home with Mum in our flat having had his usual meal which Mum had kindly prepared for him. Dad and I were chatting quite amicably about nothing in particular – I would guess it would be about the recent QPR match, as I think he missed these boys' discussions quite a lot. He asked me how I was getting on at college and then proceeded to have a go at me for not working hard at Eastbourne. Had I worked hard I would not be at college retaking exams which I should have passed at school. This had been a common gripe from Dad, one I was heartily sick of hearing. I knew my shortcomings on this topic, but he was always ready to remind me of them.

Enough was enough. I was now nineteen years old and having my father come into my home and start slagging me off yet again was too much for me to bear. My temper finally snapped and I started to lay into him, fists flying. I had him on the floor cowering in a corner. I was shouting at him that I was fed up with his constant griping and for God's sake to give it a rest.

He tried in vain to fight back but by now I was a lot bigger than him and Mum had to pull us apart, telling us we were both a couple of marauding alley cats and that she would not tolerate this kind of behaviour in her home. She was quite correct. I let Dad get to his feet and he left swiftly with his tail between his legs, giving me a look which said "How dare you?". Over the ensuing days and weeks Mum tried to get me to phone Dad and apologise for my actions, which I stubbornly refused to do. I think that she realised why I had reacted as I did, but she did not want to appear to be taking sides.

It must have been a month or so later that I happened to bump into Dad while out and about in the town shopping. We spoke to each other as if nothing at all had happened and he invited me back to his flat for a coffee which I duly accepted. We got on really well but I just got the feeling that somehow our relationship had altered. I think that for the first time he perceived me as an adult, which of course I was, and not a child. I like to think he learned this lesson a month before in Mum's flat. As time went by this proved to be true for he never, ever mentioned my school days again. Well, not in the way for which he took a mauling anyway. I am not a violent person but somehow I just lost all control that particular evening. It was years and years of the same old whining that made me flip.

It was during the month of non-contact with Mum and me that Dad spent a lot of his time back in the local pubs in Langton Green. It was as if he somehow felt at home back in the village which he knew so well, mingling with the friends and acquaintances he left behind when he moved the three miles into the centre of Tunbridge Wells. It was in one of the local public houses, The Grange, that he met a young lady who shared the same birthday as Dad. She was the daughter of a couple who had lived in the village for years, but surprisingly Dad had never met them or their daughter before, despite his long association with the village. Dad and the woman hit it off almost immediately despite an extremely large age gap. Dad was approaching sixty and she was only twenty-three, not that much older than his own son.

Tongues used to wag around the pub with utterances of disgust at the amount of attention Dad was paying to this young lady. Strangely, her parents, who always accompanied her to the pub, seemed blissfully unaware of what was going on right under their noses. At first, it was just meetings at the pub, but it soon arrived at the stage where Dad was taking her out to dinner, to a show in London or on occasions she would offer to cook him a meal at his own flat.

This was all done without her parents knowing as I am sure that if they had known that their daughter was seeing a man old enough to be her father, they would have stopped the whole thing dead in its tracks. Despite living in Langton Green, it was not until they had been seeing each other for quite a while that the young woman realised that Dad was the Subbuteo man. Now, call me cynical if you like, but from my own vantage point, their relationship seemed to take a big step forward after she realised that she was connected to Mr Subbuteo. A wealthy man, old enough to be her father. Draw your own conclusions. This reminds me of the Mrs Merton interview with the wife of a certain celebrity magician, when she was asked to explain what first attracted her to the millionaire Paul Daniels!

Within a very short space of time Dad had invited her to move into his flat. This was the first time that her parents realised what had been going on and this news went down like a lead balloon as far as they were concerned. They did not have any contact with their daughter for many months after she had moved into Dad's flat. As if shacking up with such a young woman was not cause enough for general ridicule among the people who knew him, Dad made himself more of a laughing stock by telling everyone that there was nothing in it and that she had moved in purely to be his 'housekeeper'.

He may have seen the advantage of having a young lady on hand to cook for him and to see to his laundry, but this was probably an added bonus when the invite for her to move in was given. When Mum got wind of what Dad was up to, she actually fell about laughing and made a point of phoning and telling him straight what she thought of him. A silly bugger was the phrase I believe she used.

This bizarre situation was compounded even further by the fact that I had a girlfriend at the time who was six years older than me and that made my girlfriend older than my own father's girlfriend. Quite an extraordinary situation on reflection.

I had left college by now, managing to achieve the 'O' levels I failed to get at Eastbourne, and a bit of wheeler-dealing by Dad, who greased the right palms, meant I managed to get a job working in the City for a firm of Lloyd's of London insurance brokers. It was not exactly what I wanted to do, in fact I was not quite sure what I wanted from life at this point. But it was a job after all and it paid a reasonable salary, very little of which, I am embarrassed to say, was paid to my mum by way of a contribution to the housekeeping bills at our flat.

It was at work that I met Janet who was the chairman's secretary. I moved up to Essex with her where she had a house on the outskirts of Southend. This relationship lasted only for about a year and I was soon pleading with Mum to let me back into the flat as it had all gone wrong with my time in Southend. When I left for Essex, it was very much against Mum's will for reasons which I cannot and will not go into here, and so on my departure she quite literally threw my belongings out of the third-floor flat window and told me not to come back. But mums being mums she welcomed me home with open arms. I don't think that Dad approved of my liaison with this woman, but he really did not have a leg to stand on as far as morals were concerned, so he held his tongue and kept his opinions to himself.

With an abundance of funds now at his disposal Dad thought that he would invest in some more property abroad, so he decided to sell the flat at Marina Court in Gibraltar and buy a more central property on the Rock. He also looked into the possibility of purchasing an apartment up the coast in Spain, somewhere between Gibraltar and Marbella. This was all to do with his new-found interest in the study and location of orchids which although he had been interested in botany from a young age, the specific genre of orchids was found to be an immense source of intrigue to him mainly because of their rarity value.

He had been introduced to this branch of botany by Michael Hill, a good friend of his from Tunbridge Wells, while on an ornithological trip to the Camargue region of France a few years previously. Having a base along the Spanish coast would enable him to pursue his various outdoor activities to his heart's content and so it was that he found an ideal two-bedroom apartment in a small coastal town, Torre Guadiaro, which was in the required area. It was a town which as yet had escaped the ravages of tourist development prevalent around the Marbella and Malaga area.

The flat in Gibraltar was sold for a decent profit as it turned out and he purchased another, 704 Ocean Heights, within easy walking distance of the main shopping centre, which was very convenient for him because, as in Tunbridge Wells, catering for himself was well out of the question so he was in easy reach of the vast array of restaurants and bars that were located on the main street.

The ten post-Subbuteo years for Dad were an endless round of trips to the Spanish and Gibraltar residences and numerous excursions around Europe with like-minded friends and acquaintances, indulging in his deep-set passion in ornithology and the relatively new-found interest in botany. He was certainly determined to make the best of his freedom from the day-to-day routine and, near the end, stress and strain of overseeing his beloved Subbuteo. He certainly had no financial constraints, not that there were any before really, but he did enjoy having what appeared to be a seemingly bottomless pit of funds to indulge his passions to the limit.

He would often invite me away with him on various birding trips, and I don't think he could still quite get his head around the fact that I was not as interested in his hobbies as he was, so I tended to pick and choose depending on where we would be going and which hotel we would be staying in. On some of his trips abroad, Dad sometimes stayed at the most horrendous dives you could image, purely because they were situated in a convenient location for his birdwatching.

All that mattered was that he had a bed to sleep in and reasonable food and drink to consume in the evening after a long and tiring day in the field. The ornithology and botany were the most important issues. If I did go with him, he tended to choose a more salubrious place in which to stay, like the time he invited me to go with him to Switzerland and we stayed at a typically beautiful Swiss chalet-style hotel, about thirty miles outside Zurich.

There was a chocolate-box view with cows with bells around their necks, grazing in buttercup-filled meadows, in the shadow of the most awe-inspiring snow-capped mountains imaginable. Dad's idea was that we would venture into the foothills of these beautiful mountains to explore the flora and fauna and, more importantly on this particular trip, the indigenous bird population which chose this beautiful place as their home.

Kitted out in the necessary clothing we made many trips to the said foothills but Dad was becoming increasingly agitated with me as I appeared to him to be dragging my feet on the long treks and becoming more and more tired as each day came and went. He accused me of being disinterested in the whole thing and was always having a dig at my apparent lethargy. Often the evenings were spent with neither of us saying a civil word to each other, with me sloping off to bed early because of extreme fatigue. He could not work out what was wrong with me and to be honest I was starting to be a little concerned for my own health and welfare. I was thinking that I was only nineteen years old and it was not normal for somebody of my age to be constantly lethargic and tired, some days unable to put one foot in front of the other. I eventually convinced myself that I was not all right and I voiced my concerns to Dad who more or less said that I was being a lazy so-and-so.

At long last, the time came for us to return to England, with Dad still bemoaning the fact the he did not feel that I had tried hard enough to enjoy myself on the Swiss trip, and that if he had known I was to be that faint-hearted and totally uninspired by the whole adventure, he would never have invited me in the first place, saving him a great deal of money into the bargain.

He never let up, and it was only when we got back home to England that he suggested I should visit a doctor to see if there was anything wrong with me. Blood tests revealed that I had contracted glandular fever and I was informed by the doctor that this particular condition has a very long incubation period, which goes some way to explaining the lethargy I had suffered in Switzerland. Once Dad realised this, I believe he felt guilty for having been impatient with me during this trip and he certainly tried to make amends and in his own way tried to say sorry, although that word never passed his lips. Luckily, I knew how to interpret his way of apologising, but to others who did not know him so well, his manner would have come across as uncaring. Of course he cared.

I would estimate that over the course of a year Dad would spend at least six months abroad, either in Spain or Gibraltar or just travelling. He would be away for six weeks and then return to his flat in Tunbridge Wells for a couple of weeks, where he would visit me and Mum and catch up with anything that needed his immediate attention in the UK.

He was always more than ready though to get back to his foreign abodes, as soon as possible, especially during the winter months where he could escape the ravages of this unpredictable English season. He spent Christmas mostly in Gibraltar, so I always had to be on the ball regarding his present and make sure I had something wrapped and ready for him to take to open on the big day. Sometimes this involved me thinking about Christmas in October, and at the same time finding a suitable gift for his birthday on 7th December. A nightmare. What do you buy for someone who has everything? It was always the same old story. "Just get me a nice card – that will be fine," he always used to say. He nearly always ended up with an enormous box of liqueur chocolates for his birthday and a calendar for Christmas. He adored liqueur chocolates, managing to consume a whole box in one sitting, always found a calendar useful and best of all both were easy to pack in a suitcase. Problem solved.

I firmly believe that despite severing his ties with the toys and games world in general, and Subbuteo in particular, he never lost his ability to summon up a new idea, however fanciful it might appear. After ten years or so of business inactivity, something was stirring in him. He wanted to get back on the business merry-go-round, and so it happened that, completely out of the blue, he mentioned that he felt that America was an untapped market and what did I think of coming in with him and devising a table-top baseball game?

This came as a complete shock as neither of us really knew anything about the game, apart from having seen one in New York many years before when on a family visit. I remember Dad and I loving our first experience of the American national game but that was as far as it went. At the time it never occurred to Dad that a miniature game could be attempted to be made. He must have been slipping.

We bought as many books on baseball as we could and tried to familiarise ourselves with the game's basic rules. A few of the books had to be bought in the USA and sent to England, but most were sourced from leading bookstores across the UK. However hard we tried, we found the concept of baseball hard to grasp, so with hardly any excuse needed, Dad suggested that we embark on a fact-finding trip to the States to see a few games.

Perhaps being there would help to clarify our view and understanding of the game. New York was to be our destination and we spent a week at the New York Hilton, which was very nice, and managed to see the New York Mets at the Shea Stadium in the Queens district.

Being there and experiencing the atmosphere of a top major league game, and also talking to as many people as possible about the sport, was just what we needed. Within the week we had become reasonably familiar with the basic idea of the game. I think some of the baseball fans in New York to whom we spoke, found it amusing that a couple of 'limeys' were interested in their game and even more astounded when Dad said who he was, or to be more accurate who he had been, in the context of Subbuteo, and that he was thinking of developing a baseball game. No one in New York had heard of Subbuteo then, but they made all the right noises about being familiar with the brand, but unless they had visited the UK or indeed Europe they more than likely were fibbing.

On our return home from our trip to the Big Apple, Dad decided to gather a few trusted people well known to him to help in the initial stages of planning this new game. This was to be a mammoth task, and even if a game did get into production, there would be no guarantee that it would sell in the States. We both ploughed on regardless and Dad enlisted the help of a very experienced marketing manager, David Morrison-Wilpred, who in the past worked for Subbuteo and Waddingtons and who undertook to put the whole idea on a formal footing. We formed a company called Atlantica Productions Limited with Dad, me and David as directors. The working name for the game was to be Atlantica Mini Baseball and that name eventually stuck.

Months led into years and by the early 1980s we had a prototype game up and running which, despite everyone involved being rather green in respect of playing the game, turned out to be an extremely realistic replica of the sport of baseball.

By this time, Dad had ploughed an enormous amount of his own capital into the venture, not quite knowing if he would ever see a return. By nature, prototypes of any kind always need a lot of refining to get them to a stage where they are ready for mass production and the retail market. Having spent much time number crunching, Dad got to a point where he was unable to inject any more capital, which was needed to take the game to the next level and into the toy shops across the United States.

It was getting far too expensive so it was agreed by all involved to put the project on the back burner as far as continued product development was concerned and see if sponsorship money could be raised. Companies in America were approached, but were put off by the English connection, and Dad even had the idea to write to Richard Branson himself, to see if he would be interested in some kind of sponsorship deal. I think the idea being the Virgin Atlantic connection – Atlantic, Atlantica. A tenuous thread maybe but worth a try. Dad actually received a letter back from Branson's office declining the offer to be involved in any sponsorship deal but wishing the venture every success.

After all the negative response from possible investors, and Dad's steadfast reluctance to put up any more cash for development, Atlantica Mini Baseball was put into a state of limbo for approximately ten years. Then, I believe, it was taken up again by the

David Morrison-Wilpred to see if he could do any more with it. To the best of my knowledge, he never made much of a go of it, but strangely there appears to be a limited number of Atlantica Mini Baseball games available on the internet, which are probably aimed at the Subbuteo collectors' market. One seller of the game told me he had won it as a prize in a Fantasy League Baseball competition run by Channel Five during their major league baseball coverage.

We will never know how well this product would have been received in the States had it been given a further substantial injection of funding and the correct marketing. This was to be Dad's last ever foray into the games market. How sad.

With the suspension of the Atlantica game, Dad was now able to get back into the old routine of the previous years, spending more and more of his time away from England, in sunnier climes. Now in his late sixties, he was still able to spend whole days, either on his own or with friends, walking to the most inaccessible places imaginable in search of rare orchids, which he would photograph meticulously. His photographs were always of the highest standard and I would always congratulate him on them.

He did, however, admit that sometimes the photos were not always as they seemed. He confessed to doing what he liked to call "a touch of gardening" prior to taking any photos. This entailed actually changing the environment in which the orchid was growing by setting up a different background using foliage bought in from nearby shrubs and sweeping away unwanted vegetation around the plant to create his own unique, but unnatural surroundings. These photos he often submitted to the Royal Photographic Society for judging. If only they knew.

Back in Tunbridge Wells, Mum's health was not as it should be. She was starting to find that doing the simplest of tasks would leave her extremely breathless and the doctor diagnosed an irregular heart beat and hardening of the arteries, caused mainly by smoking, but there was also, worryingly, a history of heart problems going back a few generations in her family.

I was still living at the flat in Tunbridge Wells with her at this time so I was able to help out if I could. I would juggle my time between her and my girlfriend, Nikki, who was soon to become my fiancée and then my wife on 23rd June 1984. I think that my leaving home at the ripe old age of twenty-eight was a bit of a wrench for Mum, but I have to say that Dad, when he was back in England, would look after Mum extremely well. When she was able, she quite often went to Gibraltar with Dad for a couple of weeks to get a dose of sunshine and this always seemed to perk her up.

Dad was always the exemplary host on Mum's visits to Gibraltar, and he went out of his way to ensure that she had an enjoyable stay. I don't know if this was his way of trying to make amends for his past misdemeanours or what, but I do know that, despite his murky past where other women were concerned, he never stopped loving his beloved Pam. I don't think she reciprocated these feelings, but I do know that despite everything she was still quite fond of the "old bugger" as she used to call him.

On 30th August 1985, Nikki presented Mum and Dad with their first grandchild, Lauren Victoria. They were both absolutely delighted, quite naturally, and I do believe that the new addition to the Adolph family brought them closer together. They now had a mutual interest, and as grandparents do, they spoilt Lauren to bits.

Mum regarded Lauren as the daughter I believe she always wanted, as well as myself of course, and being able to be involved with her granddaughter did help her to cope with her ever-declining health. Dad took many photos of his new granddaughter and showed them proudly to all concerned and I am sure bored his friends in Spain and Gibraltar witless with his never-ending stories of Lauren.

Their second grandchild, Thomas Mark, arrived some four years later on 5th October 1989. A male heir to keep the Adolph name alive and kicking. Dad was thrilled to be a grandfather for the second time and again, out came the camera, embarking on a second round of showing off his latest grandchild. He was mellowing in his old age.

By now Dad was heavily involved with his photography and submitting photos to the Royal Photographic Society in order to obtain his various awards, as I have detailed in a previous chapter. This was time-consuming for him and he spent hours scrutinising hundreds of his photos with a magnifying glass, trying to select the best ten for submission.

The days of thinking up new ideas for table-top sports games were well and truly behind him. Now in his early seventies, this was the passion that was driving him on. He still managed to find the time though to take long walks in the hills that lay behind the Spanish property and also walk to the top of the Rock of Gibraltar.

He was a very fit man for his age, but used to find it very frustrating if ever he became out of breath while out walking. He often phoned from Gibraltar to tell me that he had been walking up the Rock and how puffed out he had become. It was as if he could never understand why, so I had to point out every time to him that maybe, just maybe, it was because of his age. He reluctantly agreed to this fact, but I honestly believe he thought he was immune to the ravages of time and that getting old was something that happened to other people – not Peter Adolph.

The autumn of 1992 saw Mum's health take a rapid decline and she was admitted to hospital in Tunbridge Wells, barely able to walk. It was not looking good, and I had to phone Dad in Gibraltar to inform him of Mum's condition and her hospitalisation. He had not planned to come home until after Christmas, but he asked me to keep him informed of Mum's progress.

I was a little taken aback as I thought, under the circumstances, he would catch the first flight home to be near to Mum. Although he was greatly concerned, it was as if he was burying his head in the sand as far as Mum's serious state of health was concerned. The further away from the reality of the situation he was, the better. Things went from bad to worse, and Mum was discharged from hospital and admitted to a nursing home, coincidentally right next door to Dad's Tunbridge Wells flat. I knew at this point that she would never return to her own home. This was serious. Again Dad was told of Mum's transfer to the nursing home and again he refused to come home, despite my pleading with him. He was most certainly in denial about Mum but to be fair he kept in daily contact with me over the ensuing couple of weeks.

At 6 am on 4th November 1992, Mum passed away peacefully aged only sixty-two. I phoned Dad in Gibraltar to tell him the sad news. It was as if he knew why I was calling and it came as no real surprise to him, as I am sure he had been bracing himself for this news for weeks. He was, of course, devastated and asked me to let him know the funeral arrangements and he would cut his stay abroad short and come home. At last, he was reacting as I thought he should have done right from the start.

On his immediate return to England, Dad wanted to go to the chapel of rest to see Mum and asked if I would go with him. To be honest, I could not face up to that ordeal, so Nikki offered to go. I have to say that at the chapel, Dad made a laughing stock of himself by waving a crucifix over Mum and singing, in quite a loud voice, the song, 'If I Loved You', from the musical *Carousel*. The significance being that this was the show that Mum and Dad went to see on their first date together. Nikki did not know where to look she was very embarrassed, and all this in front of the attending funeral director, who I gather was trying his utmost to suppress a smile. This was very typical of Dad's overzealous manner in showing his emotion. Perhaps I shouldn't say it, but in retrospect, I do find this a rather amusing incident. Black comedy at its very best.

Mum's funeral came and went and in a strange way both Dad and I were relieved when it was all over and we could get back to something resembling normality. For two weeks or so after the funeral Dad wore a black tie, which struck me at the time as a little bit over the top. A black tie on the day, yes, but to continue wearing one weeks after the funeral was bit excessive to my way of thinking. It was as if he was trying to prove to people how much he cared. Of course he cared, and cared a lot, but this outward show of grieving did not ring true.

Up until this point in time, Dad was an extremely healthy person for a man of his years. Everything was in tip-top condition, but as soon as Mum passed away, he started getting breathless, his joints starting aching and he appeared to be suffering a small decline in his general well-being.

This worried him greatly and he went to the doctor for a general check-up. X-rays were taken and all seemed to be all right, except that he was told that perhaps it might be a good idea to cut down on his alcohol consumption, especially the red wine. Dad laughed this off, as he had no intention of cutting down. He enjoyed his drink in moderation and this action would have been the thin edge of the wedge as far as he was concerned. What pleasure was next to be outlawed?

Following his visit to the doctors, we were chatting and I don't know if this visit got him thinking or what, but out of the blue, he sat down and quite casually said to me, "If I pass out in Gibraltar or Spain, you will make sure you get me home as quickly as possible, won't you? Those people in hotter countries tend to bury you very quickly, and I want to be buried in England, not abroad." It was as if he knew. Was he having a premonition? What a lovely conversation.

Dad's general malaise was not getting any better, in fact it was getting a little worse, but he still managed to make his regular trips to his two foreign abodes. Wanting a second opinion on his worsening condition, he sought the advice of a doctor in Gibraltar whom he had visited on numerous occasions for run of the mill complaints. X-rays were again taken and this time they showed a very slight shadow on one of his lungs. He was reassured that this was nothing to worry about and that it was not unusual for a man of his age to have a small degree of discoloration of the lung, but that he must try and take things more slowly.

Not being one to give in to anything easily, let alone the small question of breathlessness and, being as stubborn as always, Dad immediately headed to Spain for a few days to check the flat and then arranged to meet a few friends and visit a favourite hotel of his, high in the mountains on the Costa Del Sol where he would spend a few days on the botany trail.

I remember it clearly as being a Monday evening in March 1994 when Dad phoned me from this hotel, and I asked him the usual questions about how he was and when he was due to come back to England. His returns to England were always eagerly awaited, for he arrived armed with cheap duty free cigarettes for me. He used to hand them over, asking politely for the money, and then give me a lecture on smoking too much and how he was encouraging me by supplying me with cheap fags.

The answers to my questions on this occasion were that he was booked to return in ten days, and that he was also feeling a bit tired, having been walking all day, up steep hills, armed with a load of camera equipment. I started to lecture him about taking notice of the doctor, and telling him that of course he felt tired. He was seventy-seven years old, with breathing problems and thinking he had the climbing abilities of a young mountain goat.

My lecture went down like the proverbial lead balloon, and he went on to tell me he was going back to Gibraltar the next morning to spend a week there before returning to England. We said our cheerios over the phone, sent each other our love and said we would be in touch later on in the week. I put the phone down. That was to be the last time I ever spoke with my dad.

Late into evening on the Wednesday, the phone rang and I assumed it would be Dad calling as he said he would. The caller was not Dad but a friend of his in Gibraltar who lived in the flat next door. She introduced herself, and I immediately remembered meeting her on one of my many visits. She told me not to be alarmed but Dad had had an accident in his flat and had been taken to the only hospital on the Rock, St Bernards.

Apparently Dad had been holding a small drinks

party for a few of the local residents and had fallen over having had too much of the vino tinto, which he should not have been drinking in the first place. He had a suspected broken hip and was being operated on as we spoke. She gave me the phone number of the hospital and suggested I phone in the morning to find out how he was.

Obviously, I slept very little that night, and first thing the following morning, 17th March 1994, I phoned the hospital in Gibraltar to find out what was happening. I was told by a member of the nursing staff, who strangely did not speak the best of English considering that most people on the Rock spoke it fluently, that Dad had had his operation the night before but was not as good as they had hoped. On asking her to be more specific, she told me in a very solemn manner that Dad was very ill indeed and things were not looking good for him. She would not elaborate any further but promised that I would be kept posted. I asked her to send him my love and hung up.

I then had this extraordinary compulsion, almost a panic, to phone his close friend Michael Hill, who lived in Tunbridge Wells, to tell him about what was happening with Dad, but I could not find his phone number. Without thinking, I jumped into the car to drive the three miles to Dad's flat in town, to see if I could find it and phone Michael from there. I know it sounds strange but I was acting as if I had no control over what I was doing. It was as if I was being guided to do what I was doing. A very odd feeling indeed. I could not find the phone number I wanted, so I decided to drive home and forget about the call I so desperately wanted to make a few moments ago.

I was halfway home again when I had this over-powering feeling that I knew for certain that Dad had died. I arrived home and Nikki was waiting for me, with tears in her eyes. All she said to me, all she needed to say to me, was, "I'm so sorry." I knew exactly what she meant. Dad had died ten minutes before and she was the one who had to take the call from the hospital in Gibraltar.

The conversation Dad and I had had just a few months ago surfaced in my mind and the poignancy of his request to be brought home immediately after his death suddenly hit home. His request was granted and within a week he was back in England. The funeral was arranged to be held at St Augustine's Catholic Church in Tunbridge Wells with a full Catholic Requiem Mass, followed by a burial in the Catholic part of the local cemetery.

Many people from Dad's past and present attended his funeral. Many business friends and colleagues came from miles around to pay their respects to the man who gave the world Subbuteo Table Soccer. Waddingtons sent as their tribute a three-foot high floral wreath in the shape of a Subbuteo figure decked out in the blue and white hoops of Queens Park Rangers.

On Dad's headstone is a simple engraving of the hobby falcon.

"FALCO SUBBUTEO"

I think that says it all.

Postscript

I AM CONVINCED that if Dad was around now, he would have been gobsmacked, for want of a better word, that Subbuteo is still alive and flicking, albeit not in the same way as it was, say, thirty or forty years ago. There are still a huge number of Subbuteo clubs and leagues, not only in the UK but also across Europe and the United States, who meet on a regular basis to play the magnificent game of Subbuteo. One only needs to enter the word Subbuteo into any internet search engine for it to display thousands of pages from across the world, all devoted to the game. There are collectors' sites and endless club and league sites, all with up-to-the-minute information on anything related to the game.

This is truly a fantastic testament to a game which will soon be celebrating its sixtieth anniversary, and is indicative of the depth of love and enthusiasm that still exists for Subbuteo, despite the now firmly established market for computer-generated games.

Dad was often asked his opinion on the future of Subbuteo when it became abundantly clear in the 1980s that these computer football games were becoming all the rage. His answer was that he truly believed there was no competition whatsoever from these type of games, and that Subbuteo was such a very well-established brand that it could easily run side by side with any computer football game.

I think he was more or less correct in his assessment, because I believe there will always be a market for a hands-on and tactile game like Subbuteo. It is just not possible to recreate this on a television or computer screen. Although, having said that, there was an alarmingly drastic downturn in Subbuteo sales, starting in the eighties, which resulted in Hasbro's announcement in 2000 that they were no longer going to produce Subbuteo any more. This caused a tidal wave of response from the general public and Subbuteo enthusiasts worldwide, so much so that in the days after the announcement, I was inundated by calls from the local and national press and local radio stations, wanting to get my views.

It was chaotic. I had no idea that Dad's game could generate such an outpouring of emotion over its imminent demise. From the people I spoke to the general feeling was that something that had become very much part of their childhood was being wiped out. In the light of this overpowering show of support for Subbuteo, Hasbro realised, I believe, that a compromise would be in everyone's interest and so decided to sell a limited amount of games and teams exclusively through the Toys r Us retail outlets. In 2005, Hasbro relaunched the Subbuteo brand on a grand scale, updating the whole concept, and in my humble opinion, keeping to the integrity and format of my dad's original concept.

Hopefully, this brand-new era for Subbuteo will introduce a whole new generation to the delights of the game, and together with everyone worldwide who still plays and loves this game, myself included, can strive to keep the name of Subbuteo going for maybe another fifty years to come. I really do hope so!

Other books from SportsBooks

Accrington Stanley - the club that wouldn't die
Phil Whalley
Accrington Stanley returned to the Football League this year after resigning in 1962. This tells the story of the years of struggle and eventual triumph.
Hardback. ISBN 1899807 47 0 £16.99

Fitba Gallimaufry
Adam Scott
Everything you need to know about Scottish football and some things you didn't.
Hardback ISBN 1899807 45 4 £9.99

All-Time Greats of British Athletics
Mel Watman
Profiles of the greatest British athletes from Walter George to Paula Radcliffe.
Paperback ISBN 1899807 44 6 4 £15.00

Ode to Jol
Alasdair Gold
A sideways, and very funny, look at Tottenham Hotspur's' 2005/06 season.
Paperback. ISBN 1899807 43 8 £12.99

Wembley – The Complete Record 1923–2000
Glen Isherwood

Every football match ever played at the world's most iconic football stadium is detailed in this exhaustive reference work.
Paperback. ISBN 1899807 42 X £14.99

Harry Potts – Margaret's Story
Margaret Potts and Dave Thomas
Harry Potts was Burnley's manager in the days the small-town team won the league and reached the FA Cup final. Great photographic section.
Hardback. ISBN 1899807 41 1 £17.99

Ha'Way/Howay the Lads
Alan Candlish
A fascinating and detailed history of the rivalry between Newcastle United and Sunderland.
Paperback. ISBN 1899807 39 X £14.99

Black Lions - a history of black players in English football
Rodney Hinds
The story of black players in English football, with interviews with players such as Garth Crooks, John Barnes and Luther Blissett. Hardback. Rodney Hinds is the sports editor of The Voice.
Hardback. ISBN 1899807 38 1 £16.99

Rowing with my Wife
Dan Williams
A year in the adventures of a gig rower, the Cornish sport that is spreading around the world.
Paperback. ISBN 1899807 36 5 £7.99

Local Heroes
John Shawcroft
The story of the Derbyshire team which won cricket's county championship in 1936, the only time the county has finished first.
Paperback. ISBN 1899807 35 7 £14.99

Athletics 2006
Editor Peter Matthews
The essential yearbook of the Association of Track & Field Statisticians and has been published every year since 1951. It contains details of the Helsinki World Championships. Previous annuals have been greatly prized by all true followers of the sport. Issues dating back to 1995 are also available.
Paperback. ISBN 1899807 34 9 £17.95

Willie Irvine – Together Again
Willie Irvine with Dave Thomas
The remarkable story of the Burnley and Northern Ireland centre forward who grew up in abject poverty, rose to the heights only to fall into depression after he stopped playing. He also found out some remarkable things about his family while researching the book, chiefly that his parents had never married!
Hardback. ISBN 1899807 33 0 £17.99

The Art of Bradman
Difficult to find a new book about the greatest batsman ever. But this is unique. A selection of paintings of the great man from the Bradman Museum at Bowral Oval with text by the museum's curator. A must for every cricket fan's collection.
Leatherbound with gold lettering and red ribbon marker.
ISBN 1899807 32 2 £25

Colin Blythe – lament for a legend

Christopher Scoble

Colin Blythe was a giant in the golden age of county cricket before the First World War. He was the most famous England cricketer to be killed in the conflict. This is the first biography of a complex personality, who was one of the first cricketers to challenge the game's rulers, demanding to handle his own financial affairs.

Hardback. ISBN 1899807 31 4 £16.99

Europe United – a History of the European Cup/Champions League

Andrew Godsell

The European Cup and its successor, the Champions League, was 50 years old in 2005 and this book celebrates all the great games and characters of the world's greatest club competition.

Hardback. ISBN 1899807 30 6 Price £17.99

Twickenham – the History of the Cathedral of Rugby

Ed Harris

The story of rugby's most famous ground, from its days as a cabbage patch to the multi-million sports arena it is now.

Hardback. ISBN 1899807 29 2 £17.99

Another Bloody Tangle!

Peter Bishop

The author loves fishing, sadly the sport doesn't reciprocate. Amazingly just before publication, Peter won his first competition and then when the cup was presented promptly dropped it. The Liverpool Echo said: "echoes of the black humour of Alan Bleasdale".

Paperback. ISBN 1899807 28.4 £7.99

The Rebel – Derek Roche – Irish warrior, British champion
Nigel McDermid

The tale of boxing hero Derek Roche is a journey from an Irish council estate to becoming the first Irishman to win a Lonsdale Belt outright. It also tells of Roche's days as a doorman in Leeds as he sought to earn a living outside the ring. The Irish Post called it a "modern classic". The Guardian said: "refreshingly honest and… genuinely funny".

Paperback. ISBN 1899807 25 X £7.99

The Complete Record of the FA Cup
Mike Collett

The ultimate statistical book on the world's oldest club competition.

Paperback. ISBN 1899807 19 3 £19.95

Are You a Proper Teacher, Sir?
Gary Boothroyd

Twenty-seven years of teaching at an inner city comprehensive school might sound like a life sentence to some, but as Gary Boothroyd found out there was a lot of fun to be had as well. His story encompasses the downright hilarious and the occasional stark tragedy. The Times Educational Supplement called it "a good light-hearted read". The Yorkshire Evening Post said: "Ten out of ten".

Paperback. ISBN 1899807 26 8 £7.99

International Rugby Who's Who
Andy Smith

This book provides all the fan needs to know about those who play the game and coach at the top level from the Zurich Premiership and Heineken Cup to the

Super 12. "An essential handbook... well produced," said the BBC.
Paperback. ISBN 1899807 23 3 £17.95

Arthur Lydiard - Master Coach
Garth Gilmour
Arthur Lydiard was probably the most successful and influential running coach of the twentieth century. Garth Gilmour, Lydiard's close friend for more than 40 years, tells for the first time the full story of the coach's amazing career, often in Lydiard's own words.
Athletics Weekly said: "a perfect tribute to an immense genius".
Hardback. ISBN 1899807 22 5 £17.99

Test Cricket Grounds
John Woods
For dedicated cricket fans who plan to watch their country play overseas. Woods spent a year and a day visiting all 58 grounds that stage Test cricket. Wisden International Cricket magazine called it "a bible for the Barmy Army... perfect..."
Paperback. ISBN 1899807 20 9 £12.99

Raich Carter – the biography
Frank Garrick
Raich Carter is the only man to win FA Cup winners' medals before and after the Second World War. Published to commemorate the 10th anniversary of his death. The Times said: "leaves the reader in no doubt about the nature of Carter's genius".
Hardback. ISBN 1899807 18 7 £16.99

Phil Tufnell's AtoZ of Cricket
Phil Tufnell with Adam Hathaway
Phil Tufnell, one of cricket's most irreverent and well-loved characters, now retired and a TV celebrity. The Cricket Magazine said: "a laugh on every page".
Paperback. ISBN 1899807 17 9 £8.99

The Complete Centre-Foward – a biography of Tommy Lawton
Another player who had his career interrupted by the Second World War, Lawton caused a huge shock when he moved from First Division Chelsea to Notts County from the Third Division, a little like Michael Owen moving to, well, Notts County now.
Hardback. ISBN 1899807 09 8 £14.99